Building for Security and Peace in the Middle East

An American Agenda

Report of the
Presidential Study Group

THE WASHINGTON INSTITUTE FOR NEAR EAST POLICY

© 1997 by The Washington Institute for Near East Policy

Published in 1997 in the United States of America by The Washington Institute for Near East Policy, 1828 L Street N.W. Suite 1050, Washington, DC 20036

Library of Congress Cataloging-in-Publication Data

Washington Institute for Near East Policy. Presidential Study Group.
      Security and peace in the Middle East: an American agenda/ Presidential Study Group; Robert Satloff, ed.
      p. cm.
      ISBN 0-944029-69-8
      1. United States—Foreign relations—Middle East.   2. Middle East—Foreign relations—United States.   3. United States—Foreign relations—1993-   I. Satloff, Robert B. (Robert Barry) II. Title.
E183.8.M628W37 1997
327.73056—dc21   97-6298
                                                                                        CIP

Presidential Study Group

Steering Group

Howard Berman
Benjamin Gilman
Alexander Haig
Max Kampelman
Jeane Kirkpatrick
Joseph Lieberman
R. James Woolsey

Co-Convenors

Robert Satloff
Samuel Lewis

Commission Members

Kenneth Adelman
Alfred L. Atherton
Graeme Bannerman
Deborah Bodlander
John Bolton
Anthony Cordesman
Paula Dobriansky
Michael Eisenstadt
Douglas Feith
Richard Haass
Bruce Jentleson
Geoffrey Kemp
Zalmay Khalilzad
Mel Levine
Alan Makovsky

Michael Mandelbaum
Will Marshall
Robert McFarlane
Daniel Pipes
Alan Platt
Kenneth Pollack
James Roche
Peter Rodman
Harvey Sicherman
Stephen Solarz
Steven Spiegel
Roscoe Suddarth
Paul Wolfowitz
Robert Zoellick
Mortimer Zuckerman

Contents

Preface

The Presidential Study Group—a bipartisan, blue-ribbon commission of statesmen, diplomats, legislators, scholars and experts—was convened in Spring 1996 to examine the state of the Middle East and the effectiveness of U.S. policy in advancing U.S. interests in that important region.

This was the third such effort organized under the auspices of The Washington Institute for Near East Policy to take advantage of election years to inject "new thinking" into the policymaking process. Previous Presidential Study Groups produced important recommendations to help guide U.S. policy toward the Arab-Israeli peace process (*Building for Peace*, 1988) and to develop the U.S.-Israel relationship (*Enduring Partnership*, 1992). At its inaugural meeting, the 1996 Study Group defined a bold and ambitious agenda—rather than focus on a single aspect of U.S. engagement in the Middle East, the group believed it essential to examine the range of U.S. interests so as to set priorities and define an overall agenda for U.S. policy.

This report is the product of that early decision. It focuses on three main regional issues (policy toward Iraq, toward Iran and toward the Arab-Israeli peace process) as well as policy toward four key bilateral relationships that are at the heart of U.S. engagement in the Middle East (U.S. relations with Israel, Egypt, Saudi Arabia/GCC and Turkey).

In the course of its nine months of deliberations, the Study Group met on a number of occasions in the offices of The Washington Institute, received extensive briefings from senior U.S. officials with responsibility for the Middle East, and engaged in vigorous discussions on the range of issues on the group agenda. Throughout, its discussions were guided by the wisdom and insight of a distinguished Steering Group that included Senator Joseph Lieberman, Congressmen Benjamin Gilman and Howard Berman, former Secretary of State Alexander Haig, Ambassadors Jeane Kirkpatrick and Max Kampelman, and former Director of Central Intelligence R. James Woolsey.

In addition, eleven members of the Study Group traveled to Egypt, Israel and Gaza in July 1996 to consult with political leaders, policymakers and analysts, representing differing views across a broad political spectrum. Especially useful were two "strategic dialogues" held separately with Egyptian and Israeli counterparts, in Hurghada and Caesaria, respectively. These retreats represented a model of how the Study Group believes bilateral communication should work with America's Middle East allies: combining candor with empathy. We thank all those in Egypt, Israel and Gaza— especially the two governments and the Palestinian Authority as well as the U.S. embassies in Cairo and Tel Aviv and the U.S. consulate-general in Jerusalem—for their assistance, cooperation and support in facilitating those retreats and the meetings with political leaders that complemented them. (Names of those who attended the Hurghada and Caesaria retreats are listed in the appendix.)

The Study Group's discussions and final report were based on and guided by "policy memos" on specific topics prepared by the following members: Graeme Bannerman, Anthony Cordesman, Bruce Jentleson, Geoffrey Kemp, Alan Makovsky, Daniel Pipes, Peter Rodman, Harvey Sicherman, and Steven Spiegel. The text of the report itself was written by Robert Satloff and edited by Samuel Lewis, Study Group co-convenors. More than twenty group members offered detailed comments on early drafts that were incorporated into this final product.

The work of the Study Group and its July 1996 trip to the Middle East were made possible by a special grant from The Washington Institute for Near East Policy. The Institute, however, had neither input nor control over the Study Group's deliberations. This report has not been endorsed by the Institute, its Board of Trustees or Board of Advisors, and it should not be taken as representing their views.

This report reflects the broad, bipartisan consensus of the members of the Presidential Study Group. Not every member endorses every judgment or recommendation. Study Group members have endorsed this report in their individual capacities and endorsements do not necessarily reflect their institutional affiliations.

A small number of recommendations provoked such deep reservations among a few group members that it was decided to reflect those views in the form of "dissenting" footnotes. These notes appear in italics at the bottom of the relevant page, with the names of the relevant group members. In the Executive Summary, points that provoked dissenting footnotes in the main text are marked with an asterisk. Given the wide range of issues addressed in the report and the diverse views of Study Group members, the small number of dissenting notes reflects a remarkably broad consensus on the fundamentals of U.S. Middle East policy.

The Study Group would like to acknowledge the invaluable assistance provided by the entire staff of The Washington Institute in organizing the group's meetings, overseas travel, and publications. In this regard, the Institute extends special thanks to Nina Bisgyer, Institute office manager; Anne van den Avond, programming coordinator; and Jonathan Torop, Steven Cook, and Lori Plotkin, rapporteurs during the July 1996 study tour and throughout our in-house deliberations.

Executive Summary[*]

A second Clinton administration faces a Middle East characterized more by challenge than by opportunity. While the signing of a Hebron redeployment accord marks a signal achievement, differences between Israel and the Arab parties suggest that prospects for major breakthroughs on the Arab-Israeli front are limited. Meanwhile, the challenges from the Gulf have grown. This change will require commensurate changes in three areas of U.S. Middle East policy: the Gulf, the Arab-Israeli arena, and in key bilateral relationships. These changes should come within the context of wider initiatives on counter-proliferation, counter-terrorism, diversification and conservation of energy resources, and the advancement of core U.S. values in foreign policy.

I SECURITY IN THE GULF

Beyond "Containment" of Iraq

The most urgent change needed in U.S. Middle East policy is to take steps that hasten the demise of Saddam Hussein's regime while preserving Iraq's national unity and territorial integrity.[*] These should include the following:

- *Clarifying declared policy on Iraq to oppose the lifting of UN sanctions or any potential reconciliation with Iraq without a regime change in Baghdad.*

- *Outlining, through a Presidential statement, a set of incentives that would accrue to Iraq's benefit in the event of the ouster of Saddam's regime.*

- *Adopting a more aggressive approach toward military responses to Iraqi provocations, commensurate with the objective of hastening the demise of Saddam's regime.[*]*

---

[*] Asterisks in the Executive Summary refer to policy recommendations that elicited dissenting comments in the main text from various Study Group members.

The Study Group recognizes the gravity of its recommendation to adopt policies designed to hasten the demise of Saddam's regime, but believes it is in the interest of the United States to clarify its objectives and take the initiative now, while its regional assets remain strong, rather than permit Saddam to determine the pace and direction of events and take advantage of the erosion of the international coalition against him.

Improving Containment of Iran: Engage with the Allies, not with Tehran

Iran poses a dangerous, long-term threat to U.S. interests. However, the Study Group believes that the lack of a coordinated policy by America and its allies poses a major challenge to even the most vigilant U.S. containment efforts. To fix this problem, we urge the United States to seek early, high-level consultations with our European and Japanese allies to achieve a common understanding regarding Iran. We urge an initiative toward Europe and Japan for an agreement that identifies definitive criteria to judge the efficacy of our allies' policy of "critical dialogue"; provides a testing period to gauge "critical dialogue" by those criteria; and then amends each side's policy following a joint review.*

In the interim, the United States should maintain its current posture vis-à-vis Iran: maximizing the cost to Iran of its continued adherence to a set of policies that constitute unacceptable behavior and that define Iran as outside the international community. At the same time, Washington should maintain its willingness to have an "authoritative dialogue" with designated representatives of the Iranian government on issues of mutual concern. The United States should be clear about the changes in Iranian behavior it seeks most to achieve through such dialogue: a cessation and renunciation of efforts to acquire or develop a nuclear capability and of further efforts to expand its weapons of mass destruction (WMDs) and delivery capabilities and an end to support for international terrorism, including the activities of surrogate groups such as Hezbollah, Hamas, Islamic Jihad and others. At the same time, the United States should be equally prepared for confrontation with Iran, especially in response to Iranian-supported terrorism against U.S. citizens, assets or interests.

II SECURITY AND PEACE IN THE ARAB-ISRAELI ARENA

The Israeli-Palestinian Peace Process: Stay the Course

Building on the recent Hebron agreement—which stipulates a process of "reciprocity" and the "parallel and immediate" implementation of past Oslo commitments to proceed concurrently with the negotiation of "final status arrangements"—the United States should remain faithful to a strategy of engagement, gradualism, and "full partnership" to advance U.S. interests in Arab-Israeli peace. In this regard, the United States should neither propose early moves to "final status" nor acquiesce in delays designed to undermine the prospects for those negotiations. *The U.S. interest in "final status" is only that it is acceptable to both parties, that it terminates the Israeli-Palestinian conflict, and that it is consistent with the U.S. position that Jerusalem should remain an undivided city. How the parties devise a formula that meets those conditions is a task for them to determine.*

In the Israeli-Palestinian negotiations, the United States should focus on fulfilling America's historic role in the peace process: nurturing an environment in which Arabs and Israelis can themselves have the mutual trust and confidence to take risks for peace. Our priorities should be to:

- *Renew the core Oslo bargain.* From the Palestinian leadership, this requires an irrevocable commitment never to resort (or threaten to resort) to "armed struggle" against Israel and to work vigorously to prevent terrorism, violence and incitement from within its ranks and territory; from the Israelis, this requires continual reaffirmation of a notion of "self-government" that has political and economic vitality, and a clear path to meaningful "final status" negotiations. A commitment to peaceful resolution of conflict is the *sine qua non* of this process.

- *Protect the integrity of Arab-Israeli agreements already made*, using the prestige of the Presidency to urge their full implementation and to monitor the parties' compliance with their contractual commitments, especially in the security realm.

- *Ensure the integrity of eventual "final status" arrangements by urging both not to "initiate or take any step that will change the status of the West Bank and the Gaza Strip pending the outcome of the permanent status negotiations."* The United States should caution against any unilateral declaration of statehood by the Palestinian Authority (PA), efforts by the PA to undertake political activity in Jerusalem, and threats by the PA to resort to confrontation or violence if its preferred "final status" outcome is not achieved. Similarly, the United States should caution Israel against punitive measures, especially in the economic realm, that have the effect of undermining self-government or eroding Palestinian support for it. As for Israeli settlement activity in the West Bank and Gaza, the United States should continue to urge maximum restraint, especially as regards the creation of new settlements, the expropriation of land for the expansion of existing settlements, and the provision of special incentives to promote settlement activity.* We urge the administration to proceed with the move of the U.S. embassy to the designated site in western Jerusalem, as mandated by U.S. law, at an appropriate moment carefully chosen to minimize its psychological impact on the negotiations.*

- *Encourage direct contact between Israel and the PA.* While U.S. mediation should always be at the service of the parties, it should not be allowed to substitute for direct dialogue, which can often have a salutary impact on the processes of reconciliation and mutual understanding that are key components of peacemaking.

- *Promote Palestinian economic development as a top priority.* The United States should offer increased technical assistance to the PA to ensure transparency and sound financial management practices that bolster donor and investor confidence; encourage Israel to lower or abolish all barriers on Palestinian exports, hasten the departure of illegal foreign workers to make room for the increased flow of Palestinian laborers who have been promised work permits in recent months, and expedite the opening of industrial parks along the "Green Line"; and urge our Arab partners to take emergency measures to assist the Palestinian economy directly and to absorb excess Palestinian labor. We urge U.S. officials to find a way to make real the promised $125 million in assistance earmarked for Overseas Private Investment Corporation (OPIC) loans and loan guarantees for private sector investment—which constitutes 25 percent of the U.S. commitment to the Palestinians—of which virtually none has been disbursed.

- *Enhance the wider regional environment for peace.* The United States should devote heightened and sustained attention to ending the virtual "freeze" on Arab-Israeli normalization that has characterized wider Arab-Israeli relations since the Israeli election, including intensive diplomatic efforts to urge Arab states that have suspended—officially or unofficially—normalization with Israel to resume the process of developing normal, bilateral relations with Israel. On this, the contributions of Egypt and Saudi Arabia are essential, and the need to bolster Jordan's own peace with Israel, critical. Now is the time for a final diplomatic push to achieve the end of the Arab boycott of Israel, once and for all.

Promoting Jordanian Stability and the Jordan-Israel Peace

Given the important U.S. interest in Jordan and the success of its peace treaty with Israel, we urge the United States to help accelerate bilateral cooperative efforts between Amman and Jerusalem, as outlined in their treaty, as well as to encourage private sector reforms that will bolster the Jordanian economy and, over time, provide the Jordanian public tangible benefits from peace with Israel. *Building on the military aid and extensive debt relief the United States has already committed to Jordan, the focus of bilateral U.S.-Jordanian efforts should be on enhancing Jordan's export capabilities and giving Jordan additional access to the U.S. market. Additionally, the United States should increase its efforts to convince other interested parties—in*

Europe, East Asia and in the Arab world—to contribute their share to the success of this peace venture. This can be done through debt forgiveness, debt rescheduling, trade credits, lowering trade barriers, and opening opportunities for Jordanian expatriate labor. In addition, we welcome the December 1996 signing of a new Jordan-Israel trade protocol that loosens trade restrictions between Jordan and the West Bank and Jordan and Israel, and we urge Israel to encourage as much westward flow of Jordanian economic activity as possible.

In the meantime, we urge the United States to pursue policies that promote Jordanian-Israeli security cooperation. Military-to-military relations are one of the brightest aspects of the still-infant Jordan-Israel relationship. Wherever possible, the United States should lend its support to joint Jordanian-Israeli military initiatives, especially in supply, maintenance, and intelligence.

Syria and the Syrian-Israeli Track of Negotiations

The United States should at all times encourage a renewal of Syria-Israel talks, on mutually acceptable terms and in a mutually agreed format, fulfilling our responsibility as "honest broker" to facilitate negotiations, exchange messages, and—if asked by both parties—to offer ideas to circumvent obstacles. While an early breakthrough is unlikely, both parties have an interest in negotiations that provide an alternative to rising tensions and the potential for open conflict that neither may be able to control. If and when negotiations resume, the United States should remain faithful to historic American positions: the path to peace remains the formula outlined in UN Security Council Resolution 242, which was the basis for Israeli and Syrian participation in the Madrid conference. How the two parties implement that resolution's call for the right of all states to "live in peace within secure and recognized boundaries" and the "withdrawal of Israel's armed forces from territories occupied" in 1967 is for them to decide.

However, the Study Group believes that the constant, high-level diplomatic engagement of the past four years is no longer appropriate. At that level of intensity, U.S. diplomacy is best invested when the opportunities for breakthrough are ripe; that is clearly not the case today. We recommend a reconfiguration of U.S. diplomacy toward Syria that entails normal diplomatic contact, at the level of assistant secretary or special Middle East coordinator, focusing on the peace process as well as the items on the U.S.-Syrian bilateral agenda: terrorism, narcotics, counterfeiting, proliferation, human rights and Lebanon. Cabinet-level trips to Damascus should be reserved for moments when the prospects of a breakthrough are high or when the potential for crisis is real. So as not to invite Syria to precipitate the latter, the United States should take all prudent measures to bolster Israel's deterrence. Out of concern that miscalculation between Israel and Syria could inadvertently lead to hostilities, Washington should urge both Damascus and Jerusalem to avoid exchanging public threats that themselves contribute to heightened military tensions.

The Study Group believes that the U.S. approach could be summarized as follows: "Washington should conduct 'normal' diplomacy toward the Syrian-Israeli track and 'intensive' diplomacy toward the Palestinian-Israeli track." That principle reflects the relative need for U.S. engagement, the urgency of the two situations, and the level of U.S. interests at stake. It suggests an emphasis on peace-building on the Israeli-Palestinian track and conflict management on the Israeli-Syrian track. We hold out the option of raising the level of U.S. engagement with Syria should the prospects of breakthrough improve.

Lebanon and the Lebanese-Israeli Track of Negotiations

With the collapse of the Soviet bloc, Lebanon has acquired the distinction of being the only satellite state anywhere on the globe. We commend a policy that campaigns internationally to end Syrian hegemony in Lebanon while working with the current government in Beirut so as to encourage incremental reforms and hold out the prospect of real independence in the future. In this regard, a lifting of the ban on travel to Lebanon by U.S. citizens is warranted. This should be accompanied by clear warnings to the governments of Syria, Iran and Lebanon that the United States will hold them responsible for ensuring that there is no renewal of hostage-taking and that the United States will react disproportionately if this warning is ignored. U.S. engagement in Lebanon should provide encouragement and assistance to those individuals and institutions working for the preservation of human rights, basic freedoms, and the rule of law. Given Syrian hegemony inside Lebanon, we urge a cessation of assistance to the Lebanese army and its redirection into humanitarian, educational and human rights efforts in Lebanon.* Throughout, we should make the implementation of the Ta'if Accord a fixture of our regional and international diplomacy and lobby our European and Arab partners to do likewise.

Renewing Multilateral Peacemaking Initiatives

The United States should seek to re-energize the Multilateral Peace Process, taking special effort to reinvigorate the arms control/regional security talks. To give the multilaterals adequate bureaucratic and diplomatic attention, we urge the appointment of a special ambassador for Middle East regional initiatives. Appropriate candidates for this position might be veterans of U.S.-Soviet arms control negotiations or accomplished leaders from the private sector.

III U.S. RELATIONS WITH ALLIES IN TRANSITION

Israel: Strengthening the Partnership

Diplomatic Coordination. Containing, managing and defusing tensions will require a renewed commitment to the concept of partnership. This means even closer coordination at the highest political levels, recognition of each party's political constraints and room for flexibility, appreciation of their overlapping but not identical strategic interests, and a persistent effort not to question the motives of the other or to provide reasons to do so. Whenever possible, communication between our two governments and their leaders should be private. The United States should also view the use or threat of punitive measures against Israel—such as sanctions, punitive cuts in economic assistance, or suspension of weapons deliveries or aspects of "strategic cooperation"—as inappropriate ways to express displeasure with particular policies; at the same time, the United States has a right to expect Israel to recognize America's broader strategic interests as a critical factor in determining its own domestic and foreign policies.

Economic Partnership. The Study Group believes that the United States and Israel are ready to transform their donor-recipient connection into a more mature partnership. Our countries should recognize as a firm objective the goal of phasing out economic assistance, the first steps toward which should be implemented within the next two years. Given that virtually all of the $1.2 billion in economic assistance goes toward repayment of Camp David-era military debt, we believe that revamping the aid program could begin by redirecting or reducing any aid funds above the amount needed for debt repayment. Options include:

- *Transferring Economic Support Funds (ESF) not used for debt repayment into military assistance.*

- *Applying ESF monies not used for debt repayment to enlarging existing binational endowments.*

- *Re-targeting those ESF monies to a special "Middle East peace fund" to support multilateral peacemaking efforts, the Middle East Development Bank, and assistance to Israel's peace partners.*

- *Deducting those ESF monies directly from overall economic assistance.* This would effectively tie the amount of annual ESF to Israel's debt, so that Israel's annual ESF never exceeds the amount of military debt repayment due each year.

Strategic Cooperation. The United States and Israel face similar, though not identical, threats from radical regimes, terrorist groups, and the proliferation of weapons of mass destruction and missile delivery systems; a particularly potent new threat is the potential use of WMDs by terrorist groups. Confronting these threats requires enhanced strategic cooperation. Here, the U.S. commitment to maintaining Israel's "qualitative edge" is critical. Specifically, we urge the two governments not only to continue joint research and development of the ARROW anti-ballistic missile program but to expand efforts to develop standardized, interoperable and effective defense systems against tactical ballistic missiles, cruise missiles and aircraft; in addition, we urge Israel's full integration into a U.S. space-based regional or global system providing instant warning of ballistic missile launching. The United States and Israel should pursue various forms of "triangular cooperation" with third countries—such as Turkey and Jordan—to build upon a congruence of interests in such areas as counter-terrorism and counter-proliferation. *As a general rule, the United States ought to help limit risks to Israel's security by making available appropriate weaponry and technology. On Israel's part, partnership entails a commitment to safeguard this technology and satisfy American sensitivities on the issue of high-tech transfer.*

Egypt: Restoring the Partnership

For two decades, the U.S.-Egyptian relationship has been a centerpiece of U.S. efforts to bolster peace and security in the Middle East. However, over the past few years, public discord and private frustration between Egypt and the United States have increased. While important areas of U.S.-Egyptian cooperation remain intact, they increasingly tend to reflect only an episodic convergence of interests, not a pattern of partnership. The Study Group believes that special attention must be devoted to building a true strategic partnership, based on a common assessment of *regional* priorities, challenges, threats and opportunities. We urge the following:

- *Creation of ongoing, high-level, bilateral consultations on political, strategic, and military matters.* The type of partnership on economic matters exhibited in the work of the Gore-Mubarak Commission needs to be extended to other areas of the bilateral relationship.

- *Deepening the U.S.-Egyptian security relationship.* It is important that the security relationship emerge from a common appreciation of regional threats and challenges.

- *Restructuring the economic relationship to promote private sector reform and U.S. private investment.* This will entail reductions in U.S. aid—not in pique and not solely in response to U.S. budget considerations, but to derive greater and longer-lasting benefit for Egypt from U.S. aid at lower cost. Now is the time to reshape the $815 million economic assistance package to bolster the process of reform, cut back the huge AID bureaucracy in Cairo, and place the bilateral relationship on a healthier footing. To do so, we urge the Administration to explore the following options: debt restructuring, replacement of aid with increased access to U.S. markets for Egyptian goods, and cuts in the AID presence in Cairo with some of the savings transferred to Egypt in the form of direct economic assistance.

We underscore the urgency for Egypt to take early action to redress the widespread perception that the U.S.-Egyptian relationship is one of periodic confluence of interests, not strategic partnership. In this regard, Egypt's policies toward Iraq and toward normalization with Israel are especially important.

Saudi Arabia and the GCC: Deepening Stability and Security

Challenges to the domestic stability of Gulf states are growing. While each faces its own unique set of problems, all share an abiding concern about the long-term impact of low oil prices, the continuing threats from Iraq and Iran, how they will manage the competing demands of each, and how they are going to pay for it. Given the closeness of U.S. political, strategic and economic ties with these states, their problems are, in many ways, America's problems, too. To help put these problems on a path toward resolution, we urge the following:

- *The United States should deepen dialogue with Gulf states on the sustainability of the U.S. military presence and on rationalizing Gulf defense expenditures.* Here, it is important for the United States to balance its desire to have Gulf countries carry the financial burden of Gulf security against the U.S. interest in the economic well-being of these countries. While Gulf states must bear their full share of expenses, they need to be encouraged to look realistically at their military needs and the importance of absorbing past purchases as they contemplate making new ones. This means the United States should not advise Gulf states to purchase equipment when they cannot afford to do so, but we should work closely with those Gulf states that have adequate resources to improve their own defenses against threats to our common interests.

- *The United States should initiate a high-level dialogue with Saudi Arabia and other Gulf states—individually and collectively—on the need for economic and social reform.* Our view is that only through structural economic reform, sound financial management, cuts in cradle-to-grave social-welfare spending and subsidy programs, and curbs on corruption that cumulatively cost Gulf economies billions of dollars do the Gulf states stand a chance of overcoming the long-term domestic challenges to their stability.

- *The United States needs to view seriously the worrying trends inside Saudi Arabia.* Among the countries in the world whose security the United States is pledged to defend, U.S. officials probably know the least about events inside Saudi Arabia. The United States needs to learn more about events and trends within Saudi society and to seek out new avenues, beyond the traditional channels of diplomatic contact, to deepen its knowledge base. This is essential if we are to offer informed advice to our Saudi allies and to safeguard our stake in Saudi stability.

Turkey: Underscoring Core Interests and Values

In its diplomacy toward Turkey, the United States faces a difficult and complex challenge: an unfriendly leader at the helm of an allied government. We believe this challenge can be best pursued through a *dual-track policy*, subtly executed, that reflects abiding U.S. interests in a stable, democratic, free-market, secular-oriented Turkey and that implicitly distinguishes between friend and foe. This policy should be guided by the following principles:

- *The United States should focus on the key issues in the bilateral relationship and avoid playing Turkish domestic politics. At the same time, the United States should not shrink from advocating its traditional support for Western values as a key component of the U.S.-Turkish relationship*

- *The United States should refrain from statements or actions that will redound to the political benefit of Turkey's Islamist movement.* The Administration should also avoid providing Prime Minister Erbakan with the symbolic victory he would enjoy from visiting Washington.[*] U.S. officials, however, should take care to maintain businesslike relations with all arms of the Turkish government, including those ministries headed by Refah partisans.

- *The United States should take special effort to maintain a strong U.S.-Turkish security relationship,* recognizing the central role that the Turkish military plays as guardian of the country's pro-Western orientation. Additionally, the United States at senior levels should make clear its support for Turkish-Israeli defense cooperation.

- *The United States should actively support closer ties between Turkey and Western Europe, as a way to anchor the Turkish state more firmly to the West.* In this regard, Washington should urge the European Union to improve ties with Ankara to keep the door open to eventual EU membership for Turkey.

Introduction

The Setting: The Middle East in 1997

As he begins his second term, President Clinton will find the Middle East far different from the Middle East of 1993. Indeed, in many ways, the circumstances that kept Middle East rejectionists at bay and permitted a great burst of Arab-Israeli peacemaking during his first term no longer obtain:

- *Russia* is no longer quietly acquiescent to U.S. dominance and instead has begun to flex its muscles through arms sales and political influence in areas of traditional interest, like the Caucasus and Iran.

- *The European Union* and key states within it, such as France, are pursuing Middle East policies increasingly independent from and at odds with the American approach.

- *Turkey*, a mainstay of the Gulf War alliance and constructive partner in the peace process, has entered a period of split government and policy drift, with the new Islamist prime minister seeking to warm ties with radical states (Iraq, Iran, Libya and Syria) while the still-powerful military establishment and secular elite remain keen to maintain close links with the United States and Europe and to develop a new strategic relationship with Israel.

- *Saddam Hussein*'s survival—in the face of coups, conspiracies, missile strikes and the UN sanctions regime—suggests that he could well outlast the U.S.-led containment, leading many states in Europe and the Middle East to begin adjusting their policies toward reconciling with Saddam, thereby accommodating a reality that was unimaginable six years ago.

- *Arab states in the Gulf*, beset by deepening socio-economic problems and uncertainties about the ability and/or will of the United States to sustain its containment strategy, are facing a period of heightened tension over their own relationships with Iraq and Iran, the high cost of defense against external threats, and the domestic political ramifications of an expanded presence of U.S. forces on Arab soil (manifested in two acts of terrorism against U.S. installations inside Saudi Arabia).

In addition to these shifts in the global environment and the situation in the Gulf, the political and diplomatic environment within the Arab-Israeli arena has changed as well.

- *Israel,* which was traumatized by a wave of Palestinian terrorism in its urban heartland and by the assassination of Prime Minister Rabin by one of its own, elected a Likud prime minister who formed a center-right/religious coalition that accepted legal responsibility for implementing the Oslo Accords but sought to re-draw the balance between the maintenance of security and the pursuit of peace in its approach to negotiations.

- *Within the Palestinian community,* as the economic situation worsened and the prospects for diplomatic progress with Israel looked bleak, both the leadership and the "street" looked opportunistically on the option of confrontation and even violence as a way to force diplomatic engagement with Israel and capitalize on the inclination of Arab and Western political and media elites to discount the Likud's commitment to peace.

- *Syria,* which had simultaneously committed itself to peace as a strategic option while supporting Hezbollah and other terrorists in their attacks against Israel and the peace process, called into doubt its own peaceful intentions by failing to grasp a generous, if conditional, offer of territorial withdrawal by the Rabin and Peres governments; since then, it has permitted the rearming of its Hezbollah proxies (following Operation Grapes of Wrath), led inter-Arab efforts to isolate the new Likud government, and undertaken military redeployments that contributed to a mini-war scare with Israel.

- *Egypt,* which paid a heavy price for its pioneering approach to peace in the 1970s and then regained inter-

Arab leadership in the 1980s without sacrificing any of its principles, has increasingly disagreed with U.S. policies and preferences. Though Cairo has fended off the most strident calls for a "freeze" in all Arab-Israel relations (e.g., hosting the November economic conference in Cairo), it has otherwise acceded to a confrontational approach toward Israel in its inter-Arab summitry, in its bilateral relationship with Jerusalem and its patronage of the Palestinians while at the same time pursuing a conciliatory approach toward terrorist-supporting states on its borders, such as Libya.

- *Jordan*, which moved quickly following the Oslo Accords to commit itself to an unprecedentedly warm peace with Israel, has grown uneasy with its role as Israel's premier Arab partner at a time when Israeli-Palestinian (and Israeli-Arab) relations are tense, when the (admittedly inflated) expectations of a "peace dividend" have yet to be realized, and when the rehabilitation of Iraq—with Saddam still at its helm—appears plausible.

- *Saudi Arabia*, which never sought a high-profile role in the peace process, has reacted to recent developments by assuming a more traditional (i.e., distant, aloof) pose, with a direct impact on the policies of the smaller Gulf states.

- More broadly, the promising process of economic relationships taking root between *Israel and Arab countries* beyond its borders has slowed, with some states— including Oman, Qatar, Morocco and Tunisia— effectively freezing their own bilateral openings with Israel and linking them to the fate of the Israeli-Palestinian relationship.

Arab-Israeli Peacemaking: Principles and Policy, 1993-96

This negative panorama contrasts sharply with the hopeful optimism that characterized America's engagement with the Middle East in the early 1990s. At that time, a confluence of events, developments and trends—American global dominance, the dissolution of the Soviet Union, cohesion in the U.S.-European alliance, the weakness of

Middle Eastern radicals and rejectionists, and a growing recognition of common interests among Israel, Turkey, and the region's moderate Arab states—presented a rare opportunity to advance U.S. national interests in Arab-Israeli peace and regional stability. Building on the sound foundation left by the Bush administration, the Clinton administration took advantage of this situation to press ahead on Arab-Israeli peacemaking based on the Madrid framework of bilateral and multilateral negotiations, while maintaining efforts to contain the radical regimes most capable of threatening regional stability, Iraq and Iran.

In terms of peacemaking, the administration committed itself to active, intensive and continual high-level engagement with an eye toward achieving contractual, bilateral peace agreements between Israel and its neighbors and to promoting intra-regional economic relations, with Israel firmly anchored in that process. *This active engagement in the peace process reflects, in the view of the Study Group, an accurate assessment of the potential contribution that a successful Arab-Israeli peace process can make to securing important U.S. interests.* Though the stakes have been lowered with the end of the Cold War and the resulting end to the danger of regional conflict escalating into superpower confrontation, these stakes nevertheless remain high. The Arab-Israeli peace process is a means to many ends: to build a community of interest among moderate states in the region in the pursuit of regional peace and stability; to help Israel achieve peace, security and prosperity; to help fulfill Palestinian political aspirations within the context of peaceful co-existence with Israel; to permit regional allies to reduce military expenditures and focus instead on economic and social development; to isolate radical states and organizations while highlighting the benefits that would accrue to them from abandoning their support for terrorism and other

---

* Dissenting Note: *Some Study Group members believe this report overemphasizes the urgency and value of U.S. "active engagement" in advancing Arab-Israeli peace negotiations and believes that when the United States does play a role in negotiations, it is wrong to serve as "honest broker," which suggests neutrality between Israel and its putative peace partners, like the Palestine Liberation Organization, that have long records of deceit and extremism (Bolton, Dobriansky, Feith, Kirkpatrick).*

unacceptable forms of behavior; and to reduce the likelihood of war at a time when its potential costs have dramatically risen due to advances in technology and the spread of weapons of mass destruction and the means to deliver them. While other countries—including America's European allies—share many of these interests and can make contributions to achieve them, we believe the United States has a unique role to play and that American participation in and leadership of the peace process is a prerequisite to its success.

For the United States, the most just, effective and lasting formula of Arab-Israeli peacemaking remains that which is embodied in the invitation to the Madrid peace conference: direct negotiations to create "real peace" based on United Nations Security Council Resolution 242. Determining the precise method to implement that resolution is a task for the parties to the dispute. Specifically, three core principles, born of three decades of American engagement in the pursuit of Arab-Israeli peace, correctly governed U.S. efforts to promote the peace process on that basis:

• The United States cannot and should not want peace more than the parties themselves.

• The United States cannot impose an agreement on the parties nor should the United States propose an "American plan" for resolution of the Arab-Israeli dispute.

• Enduring achievements are those made through direct negotiations, with America's principal contribution being to nurture an environment in which the parties themselves can reach accord and, secondarily, to advance ideas to bridge differences the parties cannot themselves overcome.

Implementing this strategy has three main components:

• *Fulfilling the responsibilities of an "honest broker" and "full partner" to the negotiations,* offering to facilitate talks, maintain the integrity of pre-arranged negotiating formats, transmit messages between parties, record hypothetical proposals, periodically propose ideas that could bridge (or at least circumvent) obstacles, and monitor compliance with contractual obligations. This is a task that only the United States can fulfill, because only the United States has the power, influence and abiding interests to help the parties terminate their conflict via a process of peaceful negotiation that provides peace, security and redress for their mutual grievances. While the United States ought not shirk from expressing its view on particular issues when its national interests are at stake, its role as "honest broker" is best implemented when it focuses as a prerequisite of success on the steady reduction of risks facing each of the negotiating partners, recognizing that they need time and a reliable political process to make the compromises essential for peace. This is especially true for Israel, given that it is being asked to make tangible compromises in terms of territory in exchange for the promise of peace and political reconciliation. At times, this American emphasis on "process" leads the parties to seek their own breakthroughs on a bilateral basis—as was the case with the secret Oslo negotiations—and when they do so freely and without coercion that is itself a success of the American concept of the "peace process."

- *Supporting, defending and protecting agreements and the peacemakers who made them,* both through direct political, financial and security assistance and via an active effort to forge an international donor coalition to do the same.

- *Insulating the peace process from threats of rejectionist regimes and terrorist groups who seek to undermine it.*

This policy has born fruit. From the Madrid peace conference through the recent signing of the Hebron redeployment protocol, Arab-Israeli peacemaking registered historic achievements, including a series of Israeli-Palestinian agreements on interim self-government, the Israel-Jordan Peace Treaty, and the convening of three Middle East/North Africa Economic Conferences. In addition, the administration invested considerable energy in promoting a difficult Israel-Syrian negotiation, which produced no breakthrough but did register some progress in terms of the depth and seriousness of the discussions.

Through it all, the administration helped sustain the process by working to insulate it from the persistent efforts of terrorists to undermine progress through violent means. Viewed *in toto*, there is no doubt that improving Arab-Israeli relations has acquired a momentum of its own, symbolized by the convening of the third Middle East/North Africa Economic Conference in Cairo in November 1996, in far less propitious political circumstances than previous such events.

In different ways, each of these achievements had an American imprint, either the result of direct American initiative or America's effort to create and nurture an environment in which the parties could themselves reach accord. That is certainly the case with the Hebron protocol. While that agreement, which was reached after months of bargaining and an outburst of violence that rocked the very foundations of the Israeli-Palestinian relationship, constitutes a hopeful starting point for further movement on the peace process, the fact that it would not have been reached without intensive U.S. mediation underscores the mistrust, suspicion and animosity which continue to plague relations between Israelis and Palestinians.

Protecting Gulf Security: Principles and Policy, 1993-96

As for the administration's second project—containment of Iraq and Iran—President Clinton also inherited a *de facto* strategy from the Bush administration, re-defined it as a policy of "dual containment," and via the increased deployment of U.S. troops in the Gulf and the imposition of an economic embargo on Iran, has applied it more broadly and forcefully.

"Dual containment" is the most recent U.S. strategy[1] to secure America's core interest in the Gulf: to ensure

---

[1] From 1972 to 1979, U.S. policy relied on the "Twin Pillars" of Iran and Saudi Arabia to ensure regional stability; this policy collapsed with the fall of the Shah. From 1980 to 1990, U.S. policy was to build-up Saudi defenses, nurture incipient defense cooperation among the countries of the Gulf Cooperation Council and, most importantly, adopt a "balance-of-power" approach toward the two other regional powers, Ba'athist Iraq and Islamist

unhindered access to the region's oil (half the world's proven reserves) and gas (one-third the world's proven reserves). Like previous Gulf security strategies, the objective of "dual containment" is to prevent any disruption of oil or gas supplies, to promote the stability of those friendly regional states which help provide access to energy resources, and to deter any unfriendly country, ideology or movement from exercising control over the region's energy resources. In this regard, it is important to recall that the danger of a regional hegemon is not only that it could restrict the flow of oil and gas, but that it could, through coercion, restore discipline to the oil cartel and thereby control the supply and price of energy as a political and economic weapon against the West. Moreover, the danger of an adversarial country exerting hegemony over the region's oil resources is also—as the Iraq case bears out—what that country can do with the vast income it would earn: namely, fund aggressive programs of conventional rearmament and nonconventional weapons development that would be used as tools of political and ideological expansionism and strategic challenge to wider U.S. interests.

In considering the need to exert U.S. leadership in the Gulf, it is also essential to recall the connection between Gulf security and the Arab-Israeli peace process. While neither is dependent on the other, the linkage between them is real: Containing Gulf rejectionists limits their political influence, ideological appeal and malicious capabilities and, in the process, gives moderate Gulf states and other regional countries the security and confidence to pursue interests in advancing wider regional stability, through such initiatives as the peace process. Conversely, fissures in America's containment strategy will have a detrimental effect on the prospects for Arab-Israeli peace.

Iran; this policy collapsed with the Iraqi invasion of Kuwait, which underscored the fact that both Iran and Iraq advance policies fundamentally inimical to U.S. (and Western) interests. Since 1990, the United States has adopted a third approach, which recognizes the sad reality about Iraq and Iran, seeks to contain and alter their aggressive policies, bolsters inter-Arab cooperative security efforts and, most importantly, projects U.S. military force into the region in an unprecedented way as the counterbalance that preserves Gulf stability.

In practice, to the extent that "dual containment" was designed to minimize the ability of Iraq and Iran to threaten immediate U.S. interests in the Gulf, this strategy has registered some success. Saddam Hussein has been kept "in a box," deprived of much of his air space, his weapons of mass destruction, his ability to import in order to re-build his army, and the regional political influence that comes with military power. Likewise, Iran has been denied its previous access to international investment and credits and has been forced to curtail spending on its conventional military build-up.

From the beginning, however, the longer-term goal of "dual containment" was to compel the regimes in Iraq and Iran to change their behavior. By this measure, U.S. policy has not succeeded. Iran and Iraq continue to engage in aggressive policies— especially the use of terrorism and the pursuit of weapons of mass destruction—that threaten regional stability and vital U.S. interests.

Moreover, during the last twelve months, there have been a series of indications that the United States will not be able to sustain even current levels of pressure against either Iraq or Iran. Iraqi resistance to the work of the United Nations Special Commission for the Disarmament of Iraq (UNSCOM), the body charged with destroying Iraq's weapons of mass destruction, is growing; at the same time, the willingness of key states to use military means, if necessary, to support UNSCOM is waning. The Iraqi opposition is in disarray; many regional states are considering a decision to reach an accommodation with Saddam; and the Iraqi armed forces are stronger now than at any time since the end of the Gulf War. On the other side of the Gulf, there is still no viable opposition to the Iranian regime despite erosion of popular support for clerical rule; the Iranian military has focused its limited acquisition budget on weapons systems, like submarines, that pose potent new threats to Gulf security; and the United States has been unable to persuade any of our European or Asian allies to join our economic embargo against Iran.

As a result, U.S. efforts to maintain (let alone tighten) containment of these two regimes has grown increasingly unilateral and therefore less compelling to the Iraqis and Iranians. This is reflected in deep differences between the United States and many of its Gulf War allies (both European and Middle Eastern) on key aspects of containment strategy. This is also reflected in the unprecedented expansion of a U.S. military ground presence in the historically closed societies of Arab states in the Gulf. One unwelcome side-effect of this U.S. presence is the growth of popular resentment against the United States and its local allies, upon which terrorists have already sought to capitalize via attacks against U.S. installations in Riyadh (November 1995) and Dhahran (June 1996). This has created the paradoxical situation in which U.S. forces are protecting themselves against terrorism from *within* countries they are there to defend as they protect those same countries from external adversaries.

The Challenge Ahead

Against this background, we believe a second Clinton administration faces a Middle East characterized more by challenge than by opportunity. The President chose to invest heavily in Arab-Israeli peacemaking in 1993 largely because the conditions for progress were ripe and our two Gulf adversaries—Iraq and Iran—were weak and contained; now both elements of that equation have changed. While the signing of a Hebron redeployment accord marks a signal achievement, fundamental differences between Israel and the Arab parties suggest that prospects for major breakthroughs on the Arab-Israeli front are limited. Meanwhile, the challenges from the Gulf have grown. This change will require commensurate changes in three areas of U.S. Middle East policy: the Gulf, the Arab-Israeli arena, and key bilateral relationships.

We believe these specific changes, outlined in the three chapters that follow, should be complemented by four broad initiatives that have special resonance in the Middle East but are truly global in scope. Each of these initiatives deserves its own Study Group report; we cite them here to underscore our collective view of their urgency, importance and centrality to U.S. strategic interests:

- *Adopt a broad-based counter-proliferation policy to deal with the most serious military danger facing U.S. interests in the years ahead—the spread of weapons of mass destruction and the multiplicity of means of delivery (ranging from ballistic missiles to terrorism).* The United States must simultaneously attempt to strengthen supplier constraints on the transfer of weapons and technology, reinforce global arms control initiatives, and support efforts to adopt regional arms control. At the same time, it must develop U.S. and regional capabilities, including effective missile defense technologies, to target and destroy enemy weapons of mass destruction, delivery systems and related facilities. It must also encourage efforts to improve passive defense measures and develop options of prevention, preemption and retaliation that will extend U.S. deterrence to help protect the region from these threats. A special focus of U.S. and international effort must be the fight against nuclear, chemical or biological terrorism.

- *Aggressively pursue counter-terrorism as a top national priority.* At home, the United States should tighten the existing set of regulations governing the access of the U.S. financial system to terrorists and their supporters and extend these regulations to all financial entities owned or controlled by terror-supporting states. Abroad, the United States should seek enhanced international cooperation to fight terrorism, to ensure that perpetrators and instigators of terrorism are brought to justice, and to prevent the recruitment, supply or fund-raising that benefits terrorist organizations. In this regard, the United States has a right to demand full cooperation from all nations in the pursuit, prosecution and punishment of terrorists (and their sponsors) who engage in acts against U.S. citizens, assets and interests; the United States also has a right to insist upon the maximum effort of all nations in preventing their sovereign territory from being used for terrorist purposes or as a transit point for terrorists.

- *Define and implement an energy policy* that seeks to limit the potentially harmful effects of instability in the Gulf by encouraging, through various market mechanisms,

expansion and diversification of sources of supply
(especially in the Caspian basin, Russia and Southeast
Asia); multiple access routes for transport of energy from
producers to consumers; and increased investment in
and incentives for energy conservation and the
development of various forms of alternative energy.

- *Articulate a policy that advocates core U.S. values—respect for the rule of law, recognition of minority and individual rights, and the value of popular participation in governance—as the basis of our consultations with friendly governments and dialogues with our adversaries.* However, ever mindful of the threat posed to the stability of friendly states by the spread of radical ideologies and militant, revolutionary political movements, the United States should not urge its allies to risk their domestic security to meet predetermined yardsticks of democratic progress.

I

Security in the Gulf

Beyond "Containment" of Iraq

To improve upon the administration's current "containment" strategy, the Study Group believes that the administration's top priority should be to take steps that hasten the demise of Saddam Hussein's regime while preserving Iraq's national unity and territorial integrity.

No single factor hamstrings the pursuit of regional peace and security as the continued survival of the regime of Saddam Hussein. While the wisdom of ending the Gulf War without requiring Saddam's removal remains disputed, there can be no dispute with the fact that the current U.S. approach was never premised on Saddam remaining in power as long as he has. As a result, the United States failed to envision the damage that even a weakened Saddam could do to an array of U.S. regional interests or the erosion of international will and unity that would undermine the effectiveness of UN sanctions.

First, Saddam has repeatedly shown he retains aggressive intentions and adequate capabilities to act on them, evidenced by Iraq's military feint toward Kuwait in October 1994 and the attack against the Kurdish-held city of Irbil in August 1996. In addition to these conventional military actions, the UN Special Commission (UNSCOM) on Iraq declared in December 1996 that Iraq continues to maintain a significant ballistic missile capability; this is in addition to the weapons of mass destruction (especially biological weapons) that UNSCOM believes Iraq has kept in hiding. Indeed, Saddam's willingness to forgo six years of oil revenue—nearly a hundred billion dollars—rather than comply with the Gulf War ceasefire requirements on weapons of mass destruction underscores the premium he places on maintaining an unconventional weapons and missile delivery capability.

Second, America's allies are growing more reluctant to respond to Iraqi provocations (such as flouting UNSCOM directives) with the seriousness they deserve. Because they do not believe the limited responses advocated by the United States have been or will be effective, some in Europe and the Middle East are concluding that it is wise to rebuild their relationship with Saddam. So many countries are losing so much money for so much longer than anyone expected that it is impossible to believe that the current situation can last indefinitely. Just days after the implementation of UN Security Council Resolution 986—"the oil-for-food" deal designed to ensure supplies of humanitarian goods to Iraqi citizens despite Saddam's refusal to comply with other UN resolutions on Iraq—many European and Middle Eastern countries began clamoring for additional exemptions to the UN sanctions regime. This is despite the fact that Saddam bears full responsibility for the hardship borne by ordinary Iraqis as a result of his capricious and vindictive behavior.[1] Against this background, the United States is likely to find it increasingly difficult to sustain the pattern of reactive and progressively more unilateral actions that characterized U.S. responses to Iraqi provocations in October 1994 and August 1996.

Third, Saddam's survival works against U.S. interests elsewhere in the region. In the Gulf, the need to maintain a sizable ground presence to deter Iraqi (and Iranian) aggression has a potentially deleterious impact on the domestic stability of host countries and on U.S.-Gulf—and especially U.S.-Saudi—relations. Put most starkly, in light of the terrorist bombings against U.S. installations in 1995 and 1996 and the deepening isolationist inclinations of the Saudi leadership, the chance that further terrorist attacks might provoke such popular outrage—either inside the United States, inside Saudi Arabia, or both—that might force an early exit of U.S. ground troops from Saudi soil cannot be entirely ruled out. In Turkey, Saddam's survival has deprived that country of up to $30 billion in trade that would normally have flowed over the Iraqi-Turkish border

---

[1] It is important to underscore that exemptions for food and humanitarian goods have been key fixtures of all sanctions resolutions against Iraq.

over the past six years; the resulting economic dislocations fueled popular discontent that helped bring the Islamist Refah party to power. In Jordan, the continued closure of (most of) the vast Iraqi market—exacerbated by the influx of Palestinian-Jordanians expelled from Kuwait and other Gulf states and the slow pace of Jordan's re-entry into Gulf markets—has hurt an economy that has yet to reap substantial benefits from its peace with Israel and the opening of the Israeli market; this is feeding opposition to the pro-peace strategy adopted by King Hussein since 1991. And as the Arab-Israeli peace process remains tense, the reintegration of Iraq into the Arab world is attracting more and more support from our moderate Arab allies as well as providing a rallying cry for those Arab states and parties keen to bolster the rejectionist cause.

Perhaps most dangerous of all, Saddam's survival is a major obstacle in the way of containing the other regime that we believe poses a significant, long-term threat to U.S. interests: the Islamic Republic of Iran. With triple Iraq's population, a more sophisticated and complex economic base, and a crucial geographic position astride the routes to both Gulf and Caspian basin energy resources, Iran is the region's great prize. If antagonistic to the West, Iran is a potent threat; if it is friendly to the West, Iran is a major asset. Under the Islamic Republic, Iran has chosen the former course, presenting a multiplicity of challenges to U.S. and Western interests—from terrorism against the peace process, to seizing UAE-owned islands in the Gulf and threatening to disrupt Gulf shipping, to promoting radical, insurrectionary movements throughout the Muslim world. Yet the more immediate nature of the Iraqi threat—Saddam has, after all, attacked four different countries since becoming Iraq's president[2]—has overshadowed the threat from Iran.

While Iran poses a dangerous long-term threat to regional stability, we reject the suggestion that containing Iran requires some form of partnership (tacit or otherwise) with the regime of Saddam Hussein. On

---

[2] These include Iran, Kuwait, Saudi Arabia, and Israel. To this list, one can add the United States, by means of the assassination attempt on former President Bush.

the contrary, the best way to contain Iran is by hastening the demise of Saddam Hussein's regime. Indeed, no single act is better designed to lead to the tightening of containment on Iran than a regime change in Iraq. An Iraq unbound by international sanctions (except those prohibiting weapons of mass destruction) will alter the regional balance of power, limiting Iranian political and military options, restricting Tehran's freedom of maneuver, and exacerbating Iran's security situation.

Similarly, we reject the notion that Saddam's demise is likely to hasten the disintegration of Iraq. In fact, the opposite is true. Saddam Hussein's continued hold on power is itself the greatest danger to the unity and territorial integrity of the Iraqi state; his ouster will almost surely help preserve that country's territorial integrity, not threaten it. With Saddam in firm control of territory only in the center of the country, both Iran and Turkey have undertaken direct military incursions into Iraqi territory, taking advantage of a vacuum-of-power in the north, as has Syria via PKK proxy. The longer Saddam stays in power, the more likely that some outside power will exploit this opportunity to create its own zone of influence or even annex a piece of territory. The best way to prevent the disintegration of Iraq—either along ethnic lines or via pieces being gobbled up by outside powers—is to have a central government in Baghdad that is able to exert authority throughout its national territory peacefully, constructively and judiciously. That can only be done in a post-Saddam regime.*

---

* Dissenting Note: *While all group members recognized the political and diplomatic utility of a U.S. commitment to preserve Iraq's territorial integrity, many questioned the principle, noting that Iraq is an artificial entity in which an Arab Sunni minority has governed—often ruthlessly—an Arab Shiite majority, while the Kurdish minority has never been accorded its promised rights to autonomy.*

An Action Plan for Iraq[*]

Operationally, a policy that seeks to hasten the demise of Saddam's regime should include the following measures:

- *The United States should clarify its declared policy on Iraq, stating categorically that it opposes the lifting of UN sanctions or any potential reconciliation with Iraq without a change in the regime in Baghdad.* This would rectify a misguided perception held by too many leaders and people in the Arab world and in Europe that the United States has become reconciled to Saddam's hold on power. That perception is a critical factor that permits Saddam to continue to hold sway over a considerable Sunni Arab constituency within Iraq; that makes Arab, Turkish and European partners hesitate to support what they perceive as half-hearted U.S. responses to Iraqi military provocations; and that helps propel Arab, Turkish and European businessmen to beat a path to Saddam's door.

  This suggested change in declaratory policy would improve upon current policy—which focuses more narrowly on the need for full Iraqi compliance with all UN resolutions—by restoring a theme that has fallen into disuse: the concept of Saddam's "irredeemability." This used to be U.S. policy;[3] if it still is, the United States should be crystal clear about it.[**]

---

[*] Dissenting Note: *Two Study Group members oppose the policy outlined herein, believing that the strategic threat posed by Iraq to U.S. interests does not now justify the risks—regionally and internationally—of pursuing a policy that actively seeks Saddam's ouster, without prior Security Council approval (Atherton, Suddarth).*

[3] As Dr. Martin Indyk, President Clinton's then-senior Middle East advisor on the National Security Council, stated in May 1993, "The current regime in Iraq is a criminal regime, beyond the pale of international society and, in our judgment, irredeemable." See "The Clinton Administration's Approach to the Middle East," in *Challenges to U.S. Interests in the Middle East: Obstacles and Opportunities*, Proceedings of The Washington Institute's Soref Symposium, Washington, DC, May 18-19, 1993.

[**] Dissenting Note: *Two members of the Study Group—who concur with the general policy of taking active measures to seek Saddam's ouster—reject the specific proposal to alter declaratory policy for fear that it would lead to a falling out among coalition partners and thereby weaken or even undermine the sanctions regime against Saddam as well as continued support of UNSCOM operations (Haass, Mandelbaum). Another member of the Study Group also supports the general policy outlined herein but notes that there is a high risk of failure and that the*

- *The United States should take all necessary measures to ensure the continued deployment of land- and naval-based U.S. forces in the Gulf, commensurate with the need to deter Iraqi and Iranian aggression and respond with overwhelming force to Iraqi or Iranian military and other provocations, as outlined below.* This includes maintenance of existing air operations in northern and southern Iraq. At the same time, the United States should take every effort to limit the exposure of U.S. forces stationed in the Gulf so as to reduce points of friction with the local population.

- *The United States should issue a Presidential statement offering a clearly defined set of incentives that would accrue to Iraq's benefit in the event of the ouster of Saddam's regime,* to complement the set of UN sanctions that will remain in force as long as Saddam and his closest associates remain in power. These incentives should include:
  — a general amnesty for all but the highest ranking members of Saddam's regime, whose continued hold on power (even in a post-Saddam regime) the United States would find unacceptable;
  — expedited removal of UN sanctions on Iraqi exports of oil and the import of non-lethal and non-dual use items;
  — amendment of the ceasefire terms to reduce the monetary damages to be deducted from Iraqi oil revenues (though not reducing the amount that would go toward funding the operation of UNSCOM); and
  — reaffirmation of the U.S. commitment to Iraq's unity and territorial integrity. In this regard, the United States should reaffirm its opposition to Kurdish independence and commit itself to recognizing the legitimate political and cultural rights of the Kurds

---

administration must quietly prepare for the slow erosion of sanctions and the prospect that Saddam may survive for quite some time (Cordesman). Additionally, he cautions that Iraq's political and strategic culture makes it highly likely that Saddam's departure will not change many of Iraq's more dangerous ambitions and actions and, as was the case vis-à-vis the Soviets during the Cold War, the United States must be prepared to deal with relatively hostile Iraqi and Iranian regimes for years to come.

only within the context of a sovereign and independent Iraq.

At the same time, the United States should make clear its view that the UN inspection and monitoring program of its WMD and missile delivery efforts will remain in place indefinitely. Here, it is important to clarify to Iraqis and the world what sort of post-Saddam regime the United States should welcome— i.e., one that respects Iraq's commitment to regional stability; that recognizes the sovereignty, territorial integrity and the inviolability of borders of all regional states; that repudiates any acquisition, deployment, use or threat of weapons of mass destruction and accepts the indefinite extension of UNSCOM's mandate to ensure Iraqi compliance with WMD restrictions; that eschews terrorism in any form for any reason and commits to prevent acts of terrorism and punish perpetrators; and that respects the legitimate rights of its Kurdish, Shi'i, Turcoman and other ethnic populations and permits their expression through political, cultural and other forms of autonomy in the framework of a unified state of Iraq. A post-Saddam regime that adopts that platform and that excludes those members of the current regime with direct responsibility for the acts of genocide, aggression and terrorism perpetrated under Saddam deserves U.S. recognition.

- *The United States should adopt a more aggressive approach toward military responses to Iraqi provocations, commensurate with the objective of hastening the demise of Saddam's regime.*[*] Increasingly, the U.S. response to provocative actions— e.g., major troop movements, violations of no-fly and no-drive zones, obstruction of UN weapons inspectors, proven complicity in terrorist acts—has been reactive in nature, limited in scope, and progressively more timid, often signalling a "more in sorrow than in anger" attitude toward Saddam.[4] Instead, these provocations

---

[*] Dissenting Note: *Two Study Group members oppose any significant military action against Iraq that lacks direct UN sanction or substantial coalition support, lest it erode Arab and other international support for the wider U.S. effort to deter Iraqi aggression against vital U.S. interests (Atherton, Suddarth).*

[4] This was the case in 1993, when the U.S. retaliated for the assassination attempt on former President Bush by bombing the Iraqi intelligence

should be viewed as opportunities to inflict as much damage as practically and logistically possible on core regime assets and personnel. Among these are the headquarters and barracks of the Republican Guard, the Special Republican Guard and the various intelligence services as well as Saddam's own military headquarters in Baghdad, Tikrit or elsewhere.

- *The United States should neither bless any particular Iraqi opposition leader nor anoint any putative successor to Saddam.* As the recent debacle in northern Iraq indicates, Washington lacks the skill, will and/or resources for clandestine efforts to engineer a coup against Saddam through cooperation with the Iraqi opposition; this is in large part a result of the lack of confidence engendered by the opposition's internecine squabbling and its lack of significant Sunni Arab (as opposed to Kurdish) support.[5] While the United States should lend political support to Saddam's opponents and insist upon the full implementation of UNSC Resolution 688, which calls upon Iraq to end its repression of the Iraqi people, we should not again permit clandestine initiatives to substitute for clarity in U.S. policy. Instead, Washington should work politically, diplomatically and militarily to create the conditions that would make regime change in Iraq more likely.

- *The United States should warn Iran against any meddling in Iraq and with Iraqi groups (such as the PUK, the KDP, or the SAIRI).* Here, it is important to underscore the U.S. commitment

---

headquarters in the middle of the night, when no senior personnel were present; in 1994, when the United States preempted an Iraqi attack against Kuwait by a rapid deployment of U.S. forces to the region that cost half a billion dollars but exacted no toll on Saddam for his threatening behavior; and in 1996, when the U.S. response to Iraq's move into northern Iraq was to launch a missile strike against anti-aircraft sites in southern Iraq and to expand the Operation Southern Watch no-fly zone northward to the 33rd parallel.

[5] Indeed, America's half-hearted efforts to support two anti-Saddam projects—the Iraqi National Congress, a coalition of Sunni Arab, Shi'i Arab and Kurdish groups operating primarily from northern Iraq, and the Iraqi National Accord, a collection of former military officers and ex-Ba'athists based in Amman—left a sad legacy that should ensure that would-be coup plotters will avoid a direct U.S. imprimatur as the figurative "kiss of death."

to Iraq's territorial integrity and to preventing any outside power from threatening it. U.S. policy should be to oppose through appropriate means any Iranian incursion into Iraq that could threaten Iraq's territorial integrity, just as the United States should oppose any entry into Iran of Iraqi-backed groups that threatens Iran's territorial integrity.

Similarly, the United States should take care to ensure that its focus on Iraq does not come at the expense of a firm U.S. posture against aggressive Iranian initiatives elsewhere in the Gulf. Geography dictates that southern Gulf states, like the United Arab Emirates and Bahrain, view Iran as their preeminent strategic threat, which has the effect of complicating U.S. efforts against Iraq. While Washington should take a firm stand against any incremental rehabilitation of Saddam Hussein, this must be backed up by vigorous and sustained efforts to support southern Gulf states in deterring Iranian military aggression and preventing Iranian political subversion.

- *The United States should undertake urgent, private consultations with European and Middle Eastern allies about the U.S. perception of the Iraqi situation,* the need to adopt a more assertive approach toward Saddam's regime as a way to save the Iraqi people from further misery and the region from further bloodshed, and the U.S. commitment to persevere with this policy until its goals are attained. Washington should work assiduously with our allies to gain their participation, support or at least acquiescence to the policy outlined above.

The Study Group recognizes the gravity of its recommendation to adopt policies—both private and public—designed to hasten the demise of Saddam's regime and does not propose it lightly. Specifically, there are strong arguments against a public declaration rejecting any possibility of reconciliation with Saddam's regime and opposing any future repeal of UN sanctions on Iraq without regime change in Baghdad. Such a policy could worsen already tense relations with our allies *vis-à-vis* Iraq. It also runs the risk of reducing Saddam's incentive for cooperating with UNSCOM and complying with Security

Council mandates, with the potential of provoking Saddam into lashing out against U.S. interests and U.S. regional allies, perhaps using missiles and weapons of mass destruction. Even if Saddam does not react militarily, this policy could redound to his political benefit by raising his stature as America's "public enemy number one." Moreover, some might suggest that at a time of relative peace, after the first full presidential term since World War II when the Middle East witnessed neither regional war nor full-scale revolution, it would be foolhardy to precipitate a confrontation with Saddam without a guarantee that the steps outlined above will bring about their desired outcome.

We believe, however, that it would be even more foolhardy to let time work against us, as our deterrent posture in the Gulf suffers from the threat of terrorism and from growing popular resentment within countries that host U.S. forces, as the international coalition against Iraq gradually erodes, and as European and Arab states progressively reconcile with Saddam. In this environment, we are convinced that the benefits of injecting clarity into U.S. policy, backed up with a greater willingness to respond forcefully to Iraqi provocations, outweigh the potential costs. *Believing, as we do, in the near inevitability of future clashes with Saddam, it is far better for the United States to clarify its objectives and take the initiative now, while its regional assets remain strong, rather than permit Saddam to determine the pace and direction of events.*

Improving Containment of Iran: Engage with the Allies, not with Tehran

As noted above, we believe that the Islamic Republic of Iran also poses a major, long-term threat to U.S. interests in the Middle East. To confront this threat, U.S. efforts to contain Iran have grown more aggressive over the last two years. They include the imposition of a total trade embargo on Iran, ending an anomalous situation in which the United States was one of Iran's leading trading partners despite our containment efforts, and the unanimous approval by both houses of Congress of the Iran-Libya Sanctions Act, imposing punitive measures against third-country entities that invest $40 million or more in Iran's (or

Libya's) energy industry. These and other U.S. efforts emerged from America's long and bitter experience with the Islamic Republic, when past initiatives to identify and strengthen "moderates" within the Iranian leadership have backfired, with disastrous results for U.S. interests.

As for the "active containment" policy of recent years, evidence suggests it has helped dissuade some allies (like Japan) from proceeding with planned concessionary loans and that it factored heavily in the decision of a number of companies to cancel or postpone investments in Iran.[6] This has contributed to some degree to the economic weakness of the Iranian regime, which limits the resources available to Tehran for military modernization and other negative purposes. However, over the past year, the successes of U.S. containment strategy have been mitigated by the increase in revenues Iran has enjoyed as a result of the unexpected rise in the price of oil.

At the same time, U.S. efforts to restrict investment in Iran have provoked a harsh reaction among many U.S. allies, who particularly view the Iran-Libya Sanctions Act as an extraterritorial violation of international trade regulations (though none has, of yet, filed a complaint against the United States with the World Trade Organization). Virtually all U.S. allies claim to share Washington's view of the threats Iran poses to Western interests—Iran's pursuit of nuclear weapons, its use of terrorism to undermine the Arab-Israeli peace process and to kill regime dissidents abroad, its support of revolutionary and radical movements in numerous Muslim countries, its aggressive military behavior in the Gulf, and its refusal to lift the *fatwa* injunction against the life of Salman Rushdie—though some harbor doubts about specific charges of complicity in individual acts of terrorism. Despite this consensus, Europe and Japan generally reject a blanket effort to "contain" Iran by denying it access to international finance and investment, which is the U.S. strategy. Instead, the official policy of Japan and the European Union (supported to varying degrees by individual

---

[6] For example, not one of the eleven projects offered by Iran at a major international investment conference in Tehran in November 1995 has been bid upon by a foreign company.

EU countries) is to pursue a "critical dialogue" with Tehran that holds out "carrots"—trade credits, concessionary loans and debt rescheduling—as a way to embolden and empower "pragmatic" elements in the Iranian regime and thereby encourage changes in Iranian behavior. Whether this policy is driven by a sincere belief in the wisdom of "engagement" as a means to affect Iranian behavior, or is merely a cover for certain Western states to maintain trade links with the Iran, is unclear; what is clear is that there are virtually no positive changes in Iranian behavior to which the proponents of "critical dialogue" can point as successes of this policy.

Having gone down the route of offering Iran "carrots" in the mid-1980s, the United States believes—rightly, in the view of the Study Group—that only a sustained policy of containment can succeed in preventing Iran from acquiring even more threatening capabilities and may, perhaps, compel Iran to alter its aggressive behavior. However, no matter how rigid U.S. sanctions may be, unilateral action by Washington can never totally deny Iran access to technology, capital and international markets. The lack of a coordinated policy by the West will undermine the most vigilant U.S. efforts. This will leave the United States on the moral high ground but facing an Iran ever more capable of exerting its negative influence throughout the Middle East.

An Action Plan for U.S.-Allied Coordination on Iran

To fix this problem, we believe it is important for the United States to seek early, high-level consultations with our European and Japanese allies to achieve a common understanding regarding Iran.[*] Despite our differences, if

---

[*] Dissenting Note: *Two Study Group members oppose this initiative on the ground that it is more likely to undermine the U.S. position than to improve it. We should always talk with our allies on this issue. However, this "compromise" will be universally regarded as an unraveling of the U.S. position, with damaging fallout in the region. As a practical matter, it will open the floodgates to investment in Iran during the review period and Iran will easily be able (by minimal compliance) to confuse the issue thereafter (Rodman, Bolton). Another member of the Study Group feels the approach advocated herein is too rigid and instead recommends an amended "carrot" and "stick" policy toward engagement with Iran that seeks to open dialogue with Tehran and ease sanctions in proportion to incremental changes in Iranian behavior, not only as a result of all-or-nothing changes (Cordesman).*

there is indeed shared concern about the challenges posed by Iran to international peace and security, then a coordinated, allied strategy should be possible.

In pursuing a coordinated strategy, one approach is for America and its allies each to compromise their current positions in order to achieve some common ground from which to launch joint initiatives on Iran. A variation of this—independent of the allies but essentially complementing their approach—advocates U.S. "engagement" with Iran but on stiffer terms than has been the case with "critical dialogue," which has had "movable goal-posts" from its inception. We reject both these approaches. Whether independent of Europe or in coordination with Europe, an "engagement" strategy would blur the very real distinctions between current European and American approaches to Iran and mistakenly signal the Iranians that United States has softened its opposition to international trade, investment, credits or assistance to the Iranian regime in advance of clear and verifiable changes in Iranian behavior.

Instead, we urge an initiative toward our allies along the following lines:

- Before Iran's scheduled presidential election in mid-1997, the United States should seek agreement with Europe and Japan on *definitive criteria by which to judge the efficacy of "critical dialogue."* Criteria should focus on verifiable changes in Iranian behavior on defined issues. These could include, for example, a cessation of all support to Hezbollah, Islamic Jihad, and Hamas and a halt to all work at the Bushehr nuclear plant.

- This agreement should be coupled with mutual commitments between the United States and its allies— at the head-of-state level—to amend each side's policy pending a review of "critical dialogue" following a twelve to eighteen month testing period.

- If such an accord is reached, then the Executive Branch should request from Congress authorization to *waive the imposition of sanctions* pursuant to the Iran-Libya Sanctions Act until the close of the testing period and the U.S.-EU-

Japan policy review. If the policy review indicates that Iran did indeed moderate its behavior based on the predetermined yardsticks, the United States will continue to waive sanctions pending another twelve to eighteen month review.

- If, however, the achievements of "critical dialogue" fail to meet the pre-approved yardsticks, *then the Europeans and Japanese will, by prior agreement, amend their own policy toward Iran* by imposing tight restrictions on concessionary loans, credits and trade with Iran. In addition, waivers on U.S. sanctions against third-country entities investing in Iran's energy sector will terminate and sanctions will be imposed retroactively from the date of the original waiver. (The latter provision is important to ensure that companies recognize the risk in attempting to "grandfather" investments in Iran during the "review period.")

In the interim, the United States should maintain its current posture *vis-à-vis* Iran: maximizing the cost to Iran of its continued adherence to a set of policies that constitute unacceptable behavior and that define Iran as outside the international community. Because the United States should always remain open to avenues that seek real, verifiable change in Iranian behavior, *Washington should maintain its willingness to have an "authoritative dialogue" with designated representatives of the Iranian government on issues of mutual concern.* Here, the United States should not shrink from the issues that should be at the top of the agenda of that dialogue; nor should it extend any special incentives to Iran to engage in such a dialogue, i.e., talks should be held without prior conditions. Indeed, given that some European countries (e.g., Germany, Denmark) are themselves facing significant public pressure to stiffen their own policies toward Iran because of egregious Iranian behavior, now is *not* the time to signal weakness to Tehran—or to Europe—by proposing a softening of the U.S. terms for dialogue.

If Iran decides to pursue such a full and frank dialogue, the United States should be clear about the changes in Iranian behavior it seeks the most to achieve: a cessation and renunciation of efforts to acquire or develop a nuclear capability and of further efforts to expand its weapons of mass destruction and delivery capabilities and an end to support for international terrorism, including the activities of surrogate groups such as Hezbollah, Hamas, Islamic Jihad and others. If there are clear and verifiable changes in Iranian behavior on these items, not just verbal commitments, then the United States should be willing to ease—gradually and incrementally—aspects of U.S. containment of Iran. One area where an easing of containment, under the right circumstances, would advance both U.S. and Iranian strategic interests would be the relaxation of U.S. opposition to financing for oil and gas pipelines from the Caspian basin countries through Iran, which would open routes for Caspian Sea oil that do not pass through Russian territory.

However, given Iran's past behavior and the prospect of an Iranian presidential election that might bring to power an even more radical leadership than the current one, *the United States should be equally prepared for confrontation with Iran, especially in response to Iranian-supported terrorism against U.S. citizens, assets or interests.* The most urgent issue is the al-Khobar bombing. If Iran is shown to be responsible for this terrorist attack on U.S. troops, we urge the U.S. to undertake a major diplomatic initiative toward our European allies, Russia and China to seek the imposition of full diplomatic and economic sanctions by the UN Security Council. Should the UN effort fail, we believe that direct military action, complemented by covert operations against the Tehran regime, would be warranted. It is important that any military response aim at targets whose loss would mean a structural weakening of Iranian military power (such as the newly acquired Russian submarines) or economic capabilities (such as major oil refineries), not pin-prick air-strikes that are aimed at relatively minor or remote sites (such as oil platforms) or constrained by the need to avoid any Iranian casualties.

Defining "Red Lines" for Russian Engagement

As the United States pursues these initiatives to improve containment of Gulf adversaries, it is important to maintain a keen watch on the regional activity—and overall strategic direction—of Russia. For many years, blocking the threat of Soviet advance into the region was a key rationale for U.S. engagement in the Middle East; since the demise of the Soviet Union, this has changed, with Moscow generally playing a constructive (or at least non-obstructive) role, acquiescing to U.S. leadership in the Gulf coalition and in the Arab-Israeli diplomacy that followed. But as Russia pursues mercenary rather than imperial objectives, points of conflict with U.S. policy in the Gulf proliferate—from Russia's increasingly cozy relationship with Saddam Hussein to its destabilizing arms sales and provision of nuclear technology to Iran. This trend, which has developed under Boris Yeltsin's relatively benign governance, would only worsen under a more aggressively nationalistic leader, with negative ramifications on U.S. interests throughout the region.

We urge U.S. officials to take advantage of the relative strength of U.S.-Russian ties to clarify to Moscow those Middle Eastern "red lines" that, if crossed, could threaten the foundation of this relationship. Here, the transfer of nuclear and ballistic missile technology is at the top of the list. It is important for the United States to undertake this exercise now so as to be prepared for even more ambitious Russian initiatives in the event Yeltsin's health takes a turn for the worse or a more nationalistic leader takes the helm in Moscow.

II

Security and Peace
in the Arab-Israeli Arena

Oslo, Hebron and the Israeli-Palestinian Negotiations

The recent signing of the protocol on Hebron provides a hopeful turning point in the pursuit of Arab-Israeli peace. That agreement, negotiated with the intensive involvement of U.S. mediators, is much more than a technical understanding on security arrangements that permits the redeployment of Israeli forces from Hebron, in accordance with previous commitments in the Oslo II accord. In the first-ever agreement between a Likud-led government and the Palestine Liberation Organization (PLO), the Hebron protocol's reaffirmation of Israel's commitment to three further phases of Israeli military redeployment in the West Bank represents the historic recognition by all mainstream political forces in Israel of the concept of territorial compromise—i.e., some form of partition of historic Palestine—as the way to resolve the century-old conflict with the Palestinians. More immediately, the Hebron protocol, together with its ancillary documents,[1] constitutes an Israeli-Palestinian agreement over the agenda and timetable that will govern their relations over the next two years, stipulating a process of "reciprocity" and the "parallel and immediate" implementation of past Oslo commitments to proceed concurrently with the negotiation of "final status arrangements." In so doing, the Hebron protocol carries with it the prospect that the second Clinton administration may witness the negotiated end of the Israeli-Palestinian conflict.

Getting there will not be easy. Israelis and Palestinians may have agreed on a procedural "road-map" and principles

---

[1] These include a U.S.-drafted "Note for the Record" and U.S. letters of assurance to the Israeli government and the Palestinian Authority.

to guide them, but they are deeply divided on substantive issues. These include differences over what constitutes compliance with past Oslo commitments;[2] disputes over the procedure for determining Israel's three "further redeployments" in the West Bank over the next year-and-a-half;[3] and fundamental disagreements over their preferred approaches to "final status arrangements." Despite the hopeful optimism of the moment, these frictions are sure to emerge with a vengeance in the months ahead.

When they do, Washington will face a critical test. Already, in the face of the tensions and violence which befell the peace process in recent months, the administration heard calls from various quarters for fundamental changes in the U.S. policy. Some urged a heightened activism to "save the process." This can take various forms, including simplistic proposals for cooling ties with Israel, using aid as a lever to pressure Jerusalem into concessions, or permitting UN Security Council debates to substitute for direct Arab-Israeli engagement. Others offered more nuanced and sophisticated suggestions to leap-frog over the remnants of self-government to the "final status" talks.[4] Still others urged retrenchment, arguing that after three years of intense engagement, this round of the peace process had run its course; when it is again ripe for progress, this argument goes, the United States should then re-engage.

The Study Group commends the administration for rejecting these ideas and persisting with a time-tested

---

[2] This is the case, for example, with the PLO's promise to amend its charter and Israel's promise to provide "safe passage" between the West Bank and Gaza.

[3] Israel, supported by the United States, argues that the extent of redeployments into "specified military zones" must be a unilateral decision, based on Israel's security needs. The Palestinians argue that the location and extent of redeployments must be negotiated.

[4] The most noteworthy statement of this position is Henry Kissinger's: "America must not let itself get embroiled in an endless guerrilla war over second-order problems. The gradualist approach heretofore pursued— which I strongly favored—has run its course. It needs to be replaced by some comprehensive statement of objectives." See *Washington Post*, November 27, 1996.

strategy of engagement, gradualism, and "full partnership" to advance U.S. interests in Arab-Israeli peace. Given America's vital interest in Israel's well-being, the special responsibility to both Israel and the Palestinian Authority the United States bears as principal patron of the peace process, the common desire of Israel and the Arab parties to maintain U.S. engagement, and the linkage of the peace process to our posture in the wider Middle East, disengagement would be irresponsible and detrimental to U.S. interests. Unlike the mid-1980s, when the peace process was dormant and the United States could focus elsewhere, today the peace process is in midstream and retrenchment would send a negative message to friends and adversaries alike; after all, while the peace process has a natural inclination to progress slowly and incrementally, it can regress quickly and precipitously when tensions rise. Moreover, both protagonists—Israel and the Palestinian Authority—want us engaged every step of the way.

Similarly, we believe it would be counter-productive for the United States to force the pace of the process to "final status" negotiations before they are ripe for progress, if not success. This will first require a mutually satisfying experience with Palestinian self-government. After all, if Israelis and Palestinians cannot implement the current deal, they are unlikely to have the political will to achieve an even more difficult one. In this regard, the United States should always urge the parties to make good faith efforts to keep to agreed timetables, such as those outlined in the Oslo and Hebron agreements, as a key aspect of their mutual commitment to implementation of their obligations to each other. Washington should neither propose premature moves to "final status" nor acquiesce in delays designed to undermine the prospects for those negotiations. While one of the parties may itself propose an early move to "final status"—and, at different points in the recent past, both have—it is not Washington's place to endorse such a call unless both do. Even then, it would be an error for the United States to stake out any particular preferences regarding the outcome of the "final status" agreement. Here, it is important to underscore that the U.S. interest in "final status" is only that it is acceptable to both parties, that it terminates the Israeli-Palestinian conflict, and that it is consistent with the U.S. position that Jerusalem should remain an undivided city. How the parties devise a formula that meets those conditions is a task for them to determine.

Instead, we believe the Clinton administration should focus on fulfilling America's historic role in the peace process: nurturing an environment in which Arabs and Israelis can themselves have the mutual trust and confidence to take risks for peace. In the current circumstances, this means taking steps to make the Oslo process work for Israelis and Palestinians alike. Only when they have confidence in the value and the functioning of the process and in the benefits they derive from it will they stand any chance of successfully bridging the wide gaps which separate them on "final status" issues.

In this context, it is useful to recall that, in 1993, Israel's Labor government and the PLO overcame historic hatreds and agreed to mutual recognition and a plan for Palestinian self-government for two basic reasons: they had built up just enough trust and confidence in the intentions of the other to take the risk and, no less important, they exhausted all other options. Today, the second condition still obtains but not the first. For both Israel and the PLO, building a vibrant and effective Palestinian self-government within the context of Israeli security remains the least bad option; neither wants a return to the status quo ante. Thus, the Likud-led government may regard Oslo as "bad then, bad now and bad in the future" but the alternatives are worse and, as his performance in the Hebron negotiations showed, Prime Minister Netanyahu views his electoral mandate as to bargain harder, not to destroy the process. For his part, Arafat has very limited choices; if self-government fails, it is far more likely that a renewed *intifada*, this time led by Arafat inside the territories, would find him back in Tunis heading an exile organization, as he fears, rather than make him president of an independent state, as he wants.

But making Oslo work requires a modicum of mutual trust and confidence that the two sides currently lack. Completion of the Hebron agreement may set the implementation of the Oslo process back on track but it does not seem to augur a new "era of good feeling" between

Netanyahu and Arafat; on the contrary, the intensive involvement of U.S. mediators in drafting language for the agreement and in guaranteeing it through side letters reflects the continued hostility and mistrust which permeates the Israeli-Palestinian relationship. *Nurturing that sense of mutual trust, to make Oslo work for both Israelis and Palestinians, must therefore be a top priority.*

The Israeli-Palestinian Peace Process: Stay the Course

The United States has an important role to play by taking initiatives that deepen peace by anchoring agreements more firmly in the political, economic and strategic self-interest of the parties. Our priorities should be to:

- *Renew the core Oslo bargain.* Though the two parties reaffirmed their previous commitments in the Hebron protocol, the United States should endeavor to elicit from each of them a more fundamental reaffirmation of the core political bargain that is at the heart of the Oslo process. From the Palestinian leadership, this requires an irrevocable commitment never to resort (or threaten to resort) to "armed struggle" against Israel and to work vigorously to prevent terrorism, violence and incitement from within its ranks and territory; from the Israelis, this requires continual reaffirmation of a notion of "self-government" that has political and economic vitality, reflected in the withdrawals and military redeployments stipulated by the Oslo and Hebron agreements, and a clear path to meaningful "final status" negotiations. *The United States should make clear to both parties that it views the mutual commitment of Israelis and Palestinians to resolve their differences only through peaceful means as the* sine qua non *for the continuation of the peace process.*

- *Protect the integrity of Arab-Israeli agreements already made,* using the prestige of the Presidency to urge their full implementation and to monitor the parties' compliance with their contractual commitments, especially in the security realm. The Hebron accord called upon each of the parties to fulfill its outstanding obligations to the other based on the principle of "reciprocity" and in an "immediate [and] parallel" fashion. For Israelis, these include implementing the three "further redeployments" in the West Bank by mid-1998; releasing security prisoners; establishing a land bridge between Gaza and the West Bank; and permitting the opening of the Gaza airport. For the Palestinians, these include completing the process of amending the PLO Charter; undertaking no political or police activities outside PA areas (e.g., Jerusalem); either incarcerating or transferring to Israeli judicial authority all criminal suspects wanted by Israel; and registering or confiscating all firearms in areas under its control. As the two parties' preferred "honest broker," the United States need not shrink from reminding Israelis and Palestinians of their responsibility to fulfill these commitments fully and expeditiously. When they don't, Washington should use its moral and political weight to press for compliance— through private *démarches* at first; through public criticism, if necessary.

- *Ensure the integrity of eventual "final status" arrangements by urging both parties to remain faithful to their Oslo commitment not to "initiate or take any step that will change the status of the West Bank and the Gaza Strip pending the outcome of the permanent status negotiations."* Though the Hebron agreement mandates the renewal of "final status" talks by mid-March 1997; it is unlikely that the two parties will begin negotiating in earnest until a considerable portion of their leftover agenda from Oslo is resolved and past commitments have been fulfilled. During this period, we believe it is important that both parties maintain restraint on words and actions, especially if the potential for a successful "final status" negotiation is to be maintained.

In particular, while the Palestinians have the right to expect negotiations to lead toward "final status arrangements" that ensure their legitimate political rights, we caution against any unilateral declaration of statehood by the PA, efforts by the PA to undertake political activity in Jerusalem, and threats by the PA to resort to confrontation or violence if its preferred "final status" outcome is not achieved. Similarly, while Israel has the right to expect American understanding for vigilant action against terrorism, we also caution against punitive measures by Israel, especially in the economic realm, that have the effect of undermining self-government or eroding Palestinian support for it. As for Israeli settlement activity, both Labor and Likud have asserted the right of Jews to settle not only throughout Jerusalem but also in "Judea and Samaria"; in response, America should continue to urge maximum restraint in settlement activity, especially as regards the creation of new settlements, the expropriation of land for the expansion of existing settlements, and the provision of special incentives to promote settlement activity, given the complications that intensified settlement activity can pose to the peace process.* Most of all, to maintain the potential for a successful "final status" negotiation we urge both parties—and the community of nations that have an interest in Israeli-Palestinian peace—to take full advantage of the opportunities offered by the interim period to actively support economic, cultural and political initiatives designed to make the idea of cooperation and coexistence meaningful for Palestinians and Israelis alike.

Perhaps the most contentious issue in "final status" talks will be the disposition of Jerusalem. Here, the United States has a strong interest in ensuring that Jerusalem be an undivided city. And since only Jerusalem's territorial boundaries, not its political status as Israel's capital, will be on the "final status" agenda, we favor the move of the U.S. embassy to the designated site in western Jerusalem, as mandated by U.S. law, at an appropriate moment carefully chosen to minimize its psychological impact on the negotiations. In the

---

* Dissenting Note: *Some Study Group members oppose any suggestion that the United States should urge Israel to show restraint in settlement activity, arguing that settlements do not impede the achievement of peace and that to suggest so pressures Israel and adds to the ideological warfare against it (Bolton, Dobriansky, Feith, Kirkpatrick).*

meantime, we believe that the design and construction process for this embassy should proceed.[*]

- *Encourage direct contact between Israel and the PA.* Over the past few months, as Israeli-Palestinian relations have worsened, the American role in Israeli-Palestinian negotiations has taken on an unprecedented depth and intensity. While "direct" Arab-Israeli talks have almost always required some form of American participation, U.S. diplomats, especially the secretary of state and the special Middle East coordinator, have become virtually indispensable to the day-to-day functioning of Israeli-Palestinian negotiations. While we applaud the persistence evidently required to help Israelis and Palestinians achieve a Hebron agreement, we believe this innovation in the U.S. role neither bodes well for the long-term success of the of the process nor for the health of the U.S.-Israeli and U.S.-Palestinian relationships. Instead, we believe the United States should make every effort to avoid becoming so entangled in the negotiations that it becomes a direct party to them. Whenever possible, Washington should urge direct contact between Israeli and Palestinian leaders. These personalities need not love each other in order to understand their respective interests and political limitations. While U.S. mediation should always be at the service of the parties, it should not be allowed to substitute for direct dialogue, which can often have a salutary impact on the processes of reconciliation and mutual understanding that are key components of peacemaking.

- *Promote Palestinian economic development.* As implementation begins on the Hebron protocol, top priority in Israeli-

---

[*] Dissenting Note: *Given the intense sensitivities of the issue, it is the view of some members of the Study Group that there can be no propitious time to move the U.S. embassy to any site in Jerusalem prior to the conclusion of Israeli-Palestinian "final status" negotiations and that the risk of doing so prematurely outweighs any potential gain (Atherton, Bannerman, Cordesman, Suddarth). In the view of another group member, while it goes without saying that the U.S. embassy will eventually move to Jerusalem, it is unrealistic to imagine there is any such thing as a "moment" that can be "carefully chosen to minimize its psychological impact on the negotiations," short of a breakthrough in final status negotiations (Rodman).*

Palestinian relations must be rapid improvement in the economic situation in the West Bank and Gaza. Action taken to bolster the Palestinian economy strengthens both Israel and the Palestinians in sustaining support for the Oslo process; failure here would undermine the minimum rationale for the entire diplomacy, i.e., that through this process the parties can improve upon the status quo ante. For America, Israel, Arab states and the wider international community, helping the Palestinian economy is one of the best possible investments in the future of peace. While we have no illusion that a healthy economy is itself the panacea to eradicate the threat of terrorism and radicalism, it will strongly contribute to that process by denying the terrorists a natural constituency of supporters. Moreover, steps to bolster the Palestinian economy fall well within the Israeli political consensus and mesh nicely with Prime Minister Netanyahu's pro-growth, free-market ideology.

Within this framework, we believe the United States should offer increased technical assistance to the PA to ensure transparency and sound financial management practices that bolster donor and investor confidence; encourage Israel to lower or abolish all barriers on Palestinian exports, hasten the departure of illegal foreign workers to make room for the increased flow of Palestinian laborers promised work permits in recent months, and expedite the opening of industrial parks along the "Green Line"; and urge our Arab partners in the region to take emergency measures to assist the Palestinian economy directly and to absorb excess Palestinian labor. However, for Washington to have standing to lobby international donors to fulfill their commitments—indeed, less than half of the $2.9 billion pledged to the Palestinians by American, European, Asian, Arab, and other donors has been disbursed—then we must make good on our own promises of economic assistance. In this difficult budgetary environment, anything less than full transparency and complete openness from the Palestinian Authority will jeopardize that assistance. But under those circumstances, the United States must fulfill its side of the bargain to the Palestinians.

In this regard, we urge U.S. officials to find a way to disburse to the Palestinians the $125 million currently earmarked for Overseas Private Investment Corporation (OPIC) loans and loan guarantees for private sector investment. This constitutes 25 percent of the United States' five-year, $500 million commitment to the Palestinians, made in the wake of the signing of the Oslo Accords. But according to *Builders for Peace*, the U.S. government-sponsored initiative to promote American private-sector investment in the West Bank and Gaza, only $1.1 million of the OPIC money has been disbursed. That is because of OPIC's strict, market-based lending requirements. We urge that the Executive Branch and Congress work together to make this "phantom commitment" become real, perhaps by finding some other vehicle to deliver the economic support that this pledge was meant to provide.[*]

• *Enhance the wider regional environment for peace.* Concurrent with this initiative to promote Palestinian economic development inside the territories, the Study Group urges the administration to devote heightened and sustained attention to ending the virtual "freeze" on Arab-Israeli normalization that has characterized wider Arab-Israeli relations since Israel's May 1996 election brought a new government to power. This is important for Israelis and Arabs alike. On the Israeli side, normalization of government-to-government, business-to-business, and people-to-people contacts with the Arab world is a useful, if imperfect, test of the Arabs' sincerity for peace—and so far, the Arab side has been found wanting. The fact that economic and trade contacts have effectively been suspended since Netanyahu's victory underscores how normalization has been conditioned by

---

[*] Dissenting Note: *One member of the Study Group believes this report does not deal adequately with the nettlesome question of whether peace and stability can be achieved without greater progress toward political pluralism and accountability as well as market competition. This question is particularly acute vis-à-vis the Palestinian Authority, where the United States should use its economic aid to encourage progress toward building free political and economic institutions. It is also relevant vis-à-vis U.S. relations with other regional countries, including Egypt, Saudi Arabia and Turkey (Marshall).*

the Arab side on a "what-have-you-done-for-me-lately" approach toward Israeli peace process policy; and the fact that the Arab boycott against Israel remains in place—even in diminished form—feeds Israeli doubts that any amount of compromise in negotiations would earn Israel the recognition and legitimacy that are essential elements of security. On the Arab side, normalization makes sound political and economic sense: Not only is it a relatively low-cost way for Arab states to entice Israel to take "risks for peace," but as the regional economic summit conferences have shown, it is a proven method of attracting the interest of the international financial and investment community to a region they normally avoid.

Specifically, we urge the administration to undertake intensive diplomatic efforts to urge Arab states (i.e., Oman, Qatar, Tunisia and Morocco) that have suspended—officially or unofficially—normalization with Israel to resume the process of developing normal, bilateral relations with Israel. Given Egypt's status as a bellwether of Arab political and economic trends, special effort should be made to encourage Cairo to inject substantially more content into its own normalization process with Israel. Saudi Arabia's contribution is also essential, given the demonstration effect of Saudi actions on other Gulf states. And now is the time for a final diplomatic push to achieve the end of the Arab boycott of Israel, once and for all. (For a discussion of the Multilateral Peace Process, see below.)

The set of priorities for U.S. policy outlined above does not break much new ground; rather, it reflects the lessons of what has worked best in America's contribution to Israeli-Palestinian peacemaking over the last three decades. But as the parties move—in fits and starts, perhaps— to "final status negotiations" that hold the potential for a peaceful end to their deep and bitter conflict, now is not the time to jettison this approach and adopt a new strategy. Now is the time to stay the course.

Promoting Jordanian Stability and the Jordan-Israel Peace

The Jordan-Israel peace treaty, signed in October 1994 at the Wadi Araba border crossing, constitutes an historic milestone of the peace process. It not only terminated the state of war along the longest Arab-Israeli frontier but it outlined a concept of cooperative, warm peace that sets a new yardstick for future agreements. For this reason alone, the United States should have a strong interest in promoting Jordan's stability and ensuring the success of the Jordan-Israel relationship. But the rationale for U.S. interest in Jordan and in helping to validate the wisdom of its peace with Israel runs deeper.

- Given that the Hashemite regime is host to a population that is predominantly Palestinian in origin, plus the fact that the Hashemites have maintained important clandestine ties with Israel that date back to the Palestine Mandate, the fate of the Jordan-Israel relationship has a direct and powerful demonstration effect on Palestinians and Israelis alike. In this regard, "making Wadi Araba work" for the Jordanians and Israelis is a key factor in "making Oslo work" for the Palestinians and Israelis.

- A vibrant Jordan permits the Jordanian leadership, including King Hussein, to fulfill a unique role in the Arab world that finds him both friend to Israel and constructive and welcome contributor to the peace process, a role he most recently played in the closing days of the Hebron negotiations.

- At a time when the rehabilitation of Iraq in Arab circles has re-emerged as a distinct possibility, a satisfactory experience with peace with Israel—i.e., one that provides Jordanians with the economic rewards that they were promised would follow soon after the signing of peace— would dull the appeal of a rejuvenated Iraqi-Jordanian commercial relationship.

So far, after two years, the results are mixed. On a state-to-state level, the Jordan-Israel relationship has proven relatively strong and resilient, with the full implementation of virtually all treaty requirements. On the popular level, however, relations have soured. Many factors have played a part: the Jordanians' inflated expectations of "peace dividends"; the Israeli government's "penny-wise, pound-foolish" approach to the bilateral trade relationship; the boycotts on trade and professional contacts instituted by Jordanian business and trade associations, aggressively promoted by Jordan's opposition political parties (especially Islamists); the permissiveness of Jordan's political leaders to the drift in popular opinion; and the general rise in regional tensions that followed Operation Grapes of Wrath in April 1996, the Netanyahu election in May 1996, and the violence surrounding the opening of the Hasmonean tunnel in September 1996.

Given the important U.S. interest in Jordan and the success of its peace treaty with Israel, we urge the United States to help accelerate bilateral cooperative efforts between Amman and Jerusalem, as outlined in their treaty, as well as to encourage private sector reforms that will bolster the Jordanian economy and, over time, provide the Jordanian public tangible benefits from peace with Israel. *Building on the military aid and extensive debt relief the United States has already committed to Jordan, the focus of bilateral U.S.-Jordanian efforts should be on enhancing Jordan's export capabilities and giving Jordan additional access to the U.S. market. Additionally, the United States should increase its efforts to convince other interested parties—in Europe, East Asia and in the Arab world—to contribute their share to the success of this peace venture.* This can be done through debt forgiveness, debt rescheduling, trade credits, lowering trade barriers, and opening opportunities for Jordanian expatriate labor. In addition, we welcome the December 1996 signing of a new Jordan-Israel trade protocol that loosens trade restrictions between Jordan and the West Bank and Jordan and Israel, and we urge Israel to encourage as much westward flow of Jordanian economic activity as possible. Tying Jordan into the economic life of Israel and the West Bank is a net gain for all three parties and, more generally, the cause of peace.

In the meantime, we urge the United States to pursue policies that promote Jordanian-Israeli security cooperation. Military-to-military relations are one of the brightest aspects of the still-infant Jordan-Israel relationship. This is reflected in the two parties' close coordination in counter-terrorism efforts and their decision not to have a third-party observer force to guarantee the implementation of their peace. Wherever possible, the United States should lend its support to joint Jordanian-Israeli military initiatives, especially in supply, maintenance, and intelligence.

Renewing Multilateral Peacemaking Initiatives

Now that the Hebron agreement has restored a sense of direction to the bilateral Israeli-Palestinian track of negotiations, we urge the administration to re-energize the Multilateral Peace Process, its constituent elements and complementary initiatives.* The United States erred in recent months in failing to take more assertive steps to prevent the erosion of the substantial gains made in the multilaterals; because of the difficulties in the bilaterals, the multilateral track suffered from relative inattention and has fallen into limbo. This is unfortunate for all parties to the process. While we recognize the linkage between the Israeli-Palestinian track and the multilaterals, it is precisely at times of stalemate on the former that it is essential to shore up achievements on the latter and maintain the numerous avenues of multilateral cooperation and communication that were opened over the past four years.

The United States should take advantage of the Hebron agreement to undo the damage of recent months and press ahead on the broad range of multilateral initiatives. This includes resumption of the five multilateral working groups and their "intersessional" activities; the establishment of Middle East trade, business and tourism associations, as called for by successive Middle East/North Africa Economic Conferences; and special collaborative initiatives focused on the "core four": Israel, the Palestinian Authority, Jordan and Egypt, especially joint projects in transportation, tourism, energy and environmental safety.

---

* Dissenting Note: *Some Study Group members express strong doubts about the wisdom of expending diplomatic effort to accelerate the Multilateral Peace Talks, believing that any regional economic projects that make sense for the parties are best pursued in more direct, less politicized forums (Bolton, Dobriansky, Feith, Kirkpatrick).*

Beyond this immediate agenda, we believe the administration should take special effort to reinvigorate one particular component of the multilaterals: the arms control/regional security talks. Through it has grown moribund over the past year, the ACRS forum had previously incorporated a wide array of Arab states in discussions with Israel on sensitive matters, leading to several tangible initiatives (such as the establishment of Regional Security Centers and secure communication "hotlines") that are unprecedented in the region. At the same time, many of the Israelis and Arabs active in ACRS participated in other, non-peace process projects—such as the NATO dialogue with five Arab states (Egypt, Jordan, Morocco, Tunisia, and Mauritania) and Israel and the European Union's "Euro-Med partnership" that included both Israel and Syria—that complemented their ACRS discussions. Together, these efforts have the potential for developing into a modest regional security organization that could institutionalize elements of security cooperation as the peace process moves incrementally but steadily toward resolution.[5] Reinvigorating ACRS, however, will require persistence, ingenuity and political will to resolve an Egyptian-Israeli dispute over the priority given to discussion of nuclear-related issues. We believe this is "do-able."

In this regard, we urge the appointment of a special ambassador for Middle East regional initiatives to serve as the focal point of all multilateral peacemaking efforts. Currently, this task is divided between the office of the special Middle East coordinator, which is the lead bureaucratic player on the peace process, and the Bureau of Near Eastern Affairs, which is responsible for all other U.S. diplomatic activities in the Middle East; the predictable result is that neither gives regional peacemaking the attention it deserves. Given the tangible contribution the multilateral talks and other regional projects can play both in nurturing a positive environment for progress in the bilateral track and in shaping a "post-peace Middle East,"

---

[5] Variations of this proposal have been made recently by British Foreign Secretary Malcolm Rifkind, Jordan's Crown Prince Hassan, Israeli leaders Shimon Peres and Binyamin Netanyahu and Turkish Foreign Minister Tansu Çiller.

raising the bureaucratic profile of the multilaterals is a short-term investment with a potentially large long-term payoff. In light of the priorities within the multilaterals, appropriate candidates for this position might be veterans of U.S.-Soviet arms control negotiations or accomplished leaders from the private sector.

Syria and the Syrian-Israeli Track of Negotiations

Since the end of the Gulf War, considerable U.S. effort has been invested in promoting Syrian-Israel peace negotiations. Behind this effort lies a clear rationale: the U.S. interest in ending the most dangerous military threat between Israel and its Arab neighbors and (once a complementary agreement with Lebanon is reached) completing the "circle of peace" on Israel's borders. In the six years since the Madrid peace conference, this effort produced significant progress,[6] without any slackening of U.S. punitive sanctions on Syria for its support to international terrorism or its role in the international narcotics trade. At the same time, Syria continued to take actions that fully merit those sanctions. They include

---

[6] Early on, Assad withdrew four preconditions for negotiations: no talks before an Israeli commitment to withdraw from the Golan Heights; no direct, bilateral negotiations; no separate Syria-Israel deal outside a comprehensive settlement of the Arab-Israeli conflict; and no formal peace treaty. Since then, he assented to four different negotiating formats (Madrid-style full delegations, one-on-one meetings between heads of delegations, chiefs-of-staff dialogues, and private retreats at Wye Plantation); compromised on long-held positions on a number of substantive points within the negotiations (on security arrangements, diplomatic relations with Israel, and the timetable for Israeli withdrawal) and sanctioned a series of public diplomacy initiatives (such as Foreign Minister Shara's interview to Israeli television and the visits to Damascus by an Israeli journalist and a delegation of Israeli Arabs) that may not have impressed Israeli public opinion but were surely significant concessions from Assad's point of view. In Lebanon, Assad quietly permitted the establishment of new security arrangements with a monitoring committee on which Syrian and Israeli military officers serve together. Further, while Assad criticized Israel's agreements with the Palestinians and with Jordan and abstained from any participation in the Multilateral Peace Talks, he did not take forceful measures to undermine them. In other ways too, Assad improved his behavior, agreeing—after much U.S. importuning—to permit the emigration of Syrian Jews.

providing support and sanctuary to terrorist organizations within Syria and inside Lebanese territory under its direct control; maintaining an active and lucrative trade in narcotics and counterfeiting; working with Iran to arm terrorist groups, coordinate their activities, undertake operations, permit them to claim responsibility from their offices in Damascus and broadcast their exploits from Syrian-based radio stations; tightening its grip over Lebanon by maintaining a massive troop and intelligence presence, engineering election results to its liking, and changing the country's demographic balance by exporting more than one million Syrian residents and laborers. In addition, the Assad regime has signaled its strategic priorities by committing an increasing share of its shrinking military budget to the acquisition and development of weapons of mass destruction, especially chemical and biological weapons, and missile delivery systems. Today, Syria's arsenal of surface-to-surface missiles can reach key military sites and major urban centers in Israel, Jordan, and Turkey. To a great extent, this gives Syria a "poor man's strategic deterrent" that compensates for its lack of a superpower patron.

Inside the peace talks themselves, Assad's claim to have made a "strategic decision for peace" was put to the test by a generous if conditional offer of territorial withdrawal by the Rabin government and was found wanting. Challenged by Israeli leaders who were apparently willing to accede to Syria's chief demand—full withdrawal from the Golan Heights—in exchange for a peace treaty that provided for adequate security arrangements and the establishment of normal, peaceful relations, Assad balked. Exactly why he did so is not clear. Some believe Assad fears the impact of peace on his grip on power; others believe Assad calculated he could get a better offer from Israel after Labor was returned to power, as was widely expected in early 1996.

Whatever his reasons, Assad's failure to take advantage of Israel's offer meant that he lost perhaps the best opportunity to retrieve territory he claims to want back. In the process, he alienated key elements within Israel and the United States that viewed the compromises and persistence necessary to maintain the Syrian-Israeli negotiation as worth the effort necessary to achieve peace. Given Assad's unresponsiveness to Rabin's offer (as well as to Peres' subsequent variation, focusing on economic cooperation) and Syria's support of and praise for terrorist attacks by radical Islamist groups in February/March 1996, it is not surprising that Israelis elected a new prime minister opposed to full withdrawal on the Golan and who brought into his coalition a new political party (the Third Way) whose sole *raison d'être* is to prevent it.

In looking toward the future of the Israel-Syria track, the United States should at all times encourage a renewal of Syria-Israel talks, on mutually acceptable terms and in a mutually agreed format, fulfilling our responsibility as "honest broker" to facilitate negotiations, exchange messages, and—if asked by both parties—to offer ideas to circumvent obstacles. While an early breakthrough is unlikely, both parties have an interest in negotiations that provide an alternative to rising tensions and the potential for open conflict that neither may be able to control. If and when negotiations resume, the United States should remain faithful to historic American positions: the path to peace remains the formula outlined in UN Security Council Resolution 242, which was the basis for Israeli and Syrian participation in the Madrid conference. How the two parties implement that resolution's call for the right of all states to "live in peace within secure and recognized boundaries" and the "withdrawal of Israel's armed forces from territories occupied" in 1967 is for them to decide. In the end, the United States should judge agreements by whether they are mutually acceptable to the parties concerned, with the U.S. role in negotiations to help parties reach agreements that achieve the overall objectives of peace, security and the irrevocable termination of conflict and the threat of violence. If they so merit, the United States should be prepared to support the parties to reach such agreements politically, financially, and through the provision of security assistance.

---

* Dissenting Note: *One Study Group member believes that a quarter-century of experience with Hafez al-Assad—from his accession to the present—shows that nothing but an "armed peace" can protect Israel's security vis-à-vis Syria as long as he remains president of that country and that the United States should not expend diplomatic effort to promote a negotiated settlement between Israel and Syria (Kirkpatrick).*

However, a review of the record of U.S. diplomacy toward Syria and Syrian-Israeli negotiations suggests that a change in the level and intensity of U.S. diplomacy is warranted. While Washington tends to have an exaggerated view of Syria's ability to exert control over other Arab actors, we believe it would be a mistake simply to ignore Syria and permit the emergence of a vacuum likely to be filled by terrorism and violence. Conversely, however appealing might be a "triple containment" policy in response to Syria's pattern of "rogue" activities, we believe that Syria does not pose the same level of threat as Iraq and Iran and that this approach would unnecessarily complicate the advancement of other U.S. regional interests. At the same time, we believe that the constant, high-level diplomatic engagement of the past four years is no longer appropriate. At that level of intensity, U.S. diplomacy is best invested when the opportunities for breakthrough are ripe; that is clearly not the case today.

Therefore, we recommend a reconfiguration of U.S. diplomacy toward Syria to reflect our desire for renewal of Israel-Syria negotiations, our interest in preventing conflict, our desire to support the re-building of Lebanon as a truly independent state, and our recognition of Syria's status as a mid-sized regional power that remains a potential partner for peace but that stands outside the international consensus of acceptable behavior on a range of key issues. In practice, this would entail normal diplomatic contact, at the level of assistant secretary or special Middle East coordinator, focusing on the peace process as well as the items on the U.S.-Syrian bilateral agenda: terrorism, narcotics, counterfeiting, proliferation, human rights and Lebanon. As is the case elsewhere in the world, cabinet-level trips to Damascus should be reserved for 1) moments when the prospects of a breakthrough are high or 2) when the potential for crisis is real and there is good reason to believe that high-level U.S. involvement would assist in defusing it. So as not to invite Syria to precipitate the latter, and thereby gain the attention of the most senior U.S. officials, it is important for the United States to take all prudent measures to bolster Israel's deterrence. This includes public diplomacy as well as enhanced security cooperation, in terms of early warning, information exchange, counter-terrorism and counter-proliferation efforts and U.S. support for Israeli-Turkish military cooperation that bolsters the security of both these U.S. allies. The Study Group is deeply concerned about the re-emergence of a "war option" in Syrian rhetoric and urges the administration to inform Damascus that the United States will not intercede to prevent Israel from responding to (or preempting) Syrian aggression.

Similarly, we are concerned about the potential for miscalculation and miscommunication between Israel and Syria that could inadvertently lead to hostilities. This is especially acute in Lebanon. There, shaky ceasefire arrangements negotiated in the wake of last April's Operation Grapes of Wrath— Israel's response to Katyusha missiles attacks on its northern towns and villages—are routinely flouted. Operating under a Syrian military umbrella, Iranian revolutionary guards assist and train various guerrilla and terrorist groups committed to killing Israeli troops and those of their South Lebanese Army ally; to infiltrate into Israel to undertake terrorist operations; and to provoke Israeli reactions that, they hope, will torpedo the peace process. Historically, Israeli governments have responded to provocations by targeting Lebanese, both combatant and civilians, as a way to force restraint on Syria and Iran. This policy has produced great suffering among Lebanese but only limited effects in Damascus and Tehran, prompting the new Israeli government to consider more direct retaliation against the local assets of those two state-sponsors of terrorist activity. This is an understandable position. However, to reduce the potential for escalating conflict, we encourage the administration to warn Syria against the danger of re-starting a proxy conflict in Lebanon and to urge both Damascus and Jerusalem to avoid exchanging public threats and counter-threats that themselves contribute to heightened military tensions.

In reviewing the two principal tracks of the peace process, the Study Group believes that the U.S. approach could be summarized as follows: "Washington should conduct 'normal' diplomacy toward the Syrian-Israeli track and 'intensive' diplomacy toward the Palestinian-Israeli track." That principle reflects the relative need for U.S.

engagement, the urgency of the two situations, and the level of U.S. interests at stake. It suggests an emphasis on peace-building on the Israeli-Palestinian track and conflict management on the Israeli-Syrian track. We hold out the option of raising the level of U.S. engagement with Syria should the prospects of breakthrough improve; conversely, if Syria is proven purposely complicit in the bombing of al-Khobar Towers (as some press reports citing Saudi sources have suggested) or in any other terrorist attack against U.S. personnel or assets, the Study Group would urge stiffer punitive measures, including seeking the imposition of economic sanctions by the UN Security Council and, failing that, overt and/or covert military retaliation by the United States. As noted earlier in the discussion of Iran, any such military response should aim at targets whose loss would mean a structural weakening of Syrian military power or economic capabilities.

While this approach to the two major outstanding tracks of the peace process may entail fewer visits to the Middle East by the secretary of state than in the past four years, that should not signal any lessening of U.S. engagement or Presidential interest in the fate of the process itself. On the contrary, the U.S. interest in Arab-Israeli peace remains strong; the prospect for progress, especially on the Israeli-Palestinian track, remains hopeful; and the need for U.S. engagement remains urgent. We believe these facts should be stated publicly at the Presidential level early in the administration's new term. *Indeed, the policy outlined here—preventing conflict, maintaining achievements, and laying the groundwork for future progress—may require the President and his secretary of state to prepare to spend about as much time on Middle Eastern issues over the next four years as during the last, though perhaps more by necessity than by choice.*

Lebanon and the Lebanese-Israeli Track of Negotiations

With the collapse of the Soviet bloc, Lebanon has acquired the distinction of being the only satellite state anywhere on the globe. Between 30,000 and 40,000 Syrian troops, plus an unknown number of intelligence agents, enforce Syrian will in a country that President Assad recently termed—on U.S. television—"an extension of Syrian territory."[7] While Syria's military presence has brought a cessation of Lebanon's fifteen-year civil war, that uneasy peace has been purchased at a very high price. Syria has subsumed Lebanon's interests in the peace process in its own, preventing Beirut from pursuing any substantive exchange with Israel and even denying it the opportunity to benefit from the multilateral peace process and the annual regional economic summits. Moreover, Syria has mastered the art of exploiting Lebanese political movements as proxies in its war of attrition against Israeli forces in the south Lebanon security zone. As a result, Syria's own border with Israel has been quiet for more than two decades while Lebanon's has been the setting for continual conflict and bloodshed.

Against this background, it is sadly evident that a "Lebanon first" initiative of seeking a negotiated withdrawal of Israeli forces from Lebanese territory and the creation of border security arrangements cannot succeed against Syria's wishes. Any serious discussion of improving Israel-Lebanon border security and Israeli withdrawal from the south Lebanon security zone must, by force of circumstance, take place in the context of larger Israel-Syrian negotiations. It can be the first item on the agenda of those talks, but it cannot be the only item.

A different approach envisions Israel undertaking a unilateral withdrawal from south Lebanon as the quickest way to restore calm to the Israel-Lebanon border. We believe, however, that a negotiated agreement that defines each party's duties and responsibilities is the best route to achieving security. *Therefore, we urge the administration to reject calls from some quarters for the United States to urge Israel to withdraw unilaterally from South Lebanon as a way to pacify the Israel-Lebanon border.* Israel may choose to adopt this policy on its own in order to resolve its Lebanon dilemma, but this should be the outcome of its own internal deliberations, not as a result of U.S. advocacy.

In the meantime, the United States faces a dilemma as to its approach toward Lebanon itself—whether to treat the Hrawi-Hariri government solely as a Syrian puppet regime,

---

[7] Assad interview with Rowland Evans, CNN, September 25, 1996.

denying it the legitimacy that goes with diplomatic relations, economic assistance, etc., or to pursue a more difficult and sensitive diplomatic effort of campaigning internationally against Syrian hegemony in Lebanon while working with the current government in Beirut so as to encourage incremental reforms and hold out the prospect of real independence in the future. We commend the latter course. *Despite the severe restrictions on political freedom inside Lebanon, we believe the cause of Lebanon's independence and territorial integrity is best served through sustained U.S. engagement with the people and institutions of Lebanon. This would help focus international attention on Lebanon as a way to prevent Syria's creeping annexation of that country.*

In this regard, we believe a lifting of the ban on travel to Lebanon by U.S. citizens is warranted. The travel ban made sense at a time when Americans were regularly being abducted, with the tacit (if not explicit) approval of Lebanon's Syrian occupiers. Today, with the Lebanese (and, indirectly, the Syrians) reaping the benefits of significant American and international investment in Lebanon's post-war reconstruction, thousands of American citizens are circumventing the travel ban and visiting Lebanon without falling prey to hostage-takers. In this context, maintaining the travel ban is outdated. If it is meant to signal disapproval of the Syrian occupation, there are surely more effective ways to show our views. Any lifting of the ban, however, should be accompanied by an official statement to U.S. citizens about the potential danger of travel to Lebanon as well as by clear warnings to the governments of Syria, Iran and Lebanon that we will hold them responsible for ensuring that there is no hostage-taking by Hezbollah or other groups and that the United States will react disproportionately if this warning is ignored.

As a true "friend of Lebanon," U.S. engagement should extend beyond public and private support for Lebanon's economic revitalization, however. Through academic and professional exchange programs, American educational institutions in Lebanon and the work of America's democracy-promoting foundations, the United States should provide encouragement and assistance to those individuals and institutions working for the preservation of human rights, basic freedoms and the rule of law. And while the United States has an interest in the development of a Lebanese army capable of ensuring security throughout the country, it is folly to believe that can occur while the massive Syrian troop presence in Lebanon remains in place; *we urge, therefore, a cessation of assistance to the Lebanese army and its redirection into humanitarian, human rights and educational efforts in Lebanon.** Throughout, we believe the full implementation of the Ta'if Accord, especially its provisions for the redeployment of Syrian troops outside Beirut and then outside Lebanon, is an essential step in this process. *We should, therefore, make Ta'if's full implementation a fixture of our regional and international diplomacy and lobby our European and Arab partners to do likewise.*

---

* Dissenting Note: *Two Study Group members oppose a cessation of assistance to the Lebanese Army. They believe that Lebanon cannot achieve stable independence without a better armed forces and that the United States should therefore provide appropriate military assistance, carefully designed to strengthen the army's ability to support internal security and advance national unity (Cordesman, Suddarth). Additionally, one opposes channeling U.S. assistance to humanitarian and human rights efforts, because of the likelihood of corruption (Cordesman).*

III

U.S. Relations with Allies in Transition

In addition to policies directed at two major Middle Eastern sub-regions, the Gulf and the Arab-Israeli arena, we believe the United States should devote considerable energy over the next four years to bolstering critical relationships with four major regional allies: Israel, Egypt, Saudi Arabia and Turkey. Each of these allies is undergoing a process of political, economic and social change. Focusing on these bilateral relationships, which are at the heart of our Middle East policy, deserves high priority.

Israel: Strengthening the Partnership

As the era of "heroic peacemaking" gives way to the no less important tasks of "peace building" and "conflict management," the coming period provides ample opportunity—as well as ample urgency—for the United States and Israel to strengthen their bilateral partnership in the political, economic and strategic realms:

Diplomatic Coordination. The Hebron agreement once again reaffirms the wisdom of close coordination with Israel as a key to progress in the peace process. This remains essential, though admittedly more sensitive and difficult, when Israel and the United States advocate different policies on specific issues in the negotiations. As we approach the next set of items on the peace process agenda, there is no hiding the fact that the new Israeli government advocates policies in some areas—from its view of the future disposition of the Golan Heights to settlement policy in the West Bank—that run counter to declared U.S. policy. This does not mean, however, that the U.S.-Israel relationship is headed for a rerun of the Bush-Shamir tensions. We believe the U.S.-Israeli partnership has matured beyond the point at which disagreements about specific items in the peace process need to infect the entire web of relationships that constitute this alliance.

Containing, managing and defusing tensions will require a renewed commitment to the very concept of partnership. It means more than just respect for the concept of "no surprises." This means even closer coordination at the highest political levels, recognition of each party's political constraints and room for flexibility, appreciation of their overlapping but not identical strategic interests, and a persistent effort not to question each other's motives or provide reasons to do so.

Communication between our two governments and their leaders should, whenever possible, be private, befitting the closeness of the relationship and the common goals we share; however, there are still likely to be moments when public statements to reinforce private concerns may be necessary. In this regard, the United States should persistently oppose the introduction of the United Nations into Arab-Israeli diplomacy, in the belief that direct Arab-Israeli negotiations are the best way to resolve outstanding disputes. The United States should also view the use or threat of punitive measures against Israel—such as sanctions, punitive cuts in economic assistance, or suspension of weapons deliveries or aspects of "strategic cooperation"—as inappropriate ways to express displeasure with particular policies, given the important role that the U.S.-Israeli relationship plays in Israel's deterrent posture; at the same time, the United States has a right to expect Israel to recognize America's broader strategic interests as a critical factor in determining its own domestic and foreign policies.

Through it all, it is important to remember that it was under a Likud government that the peace process recorded two of its most important achievements—the Egypt-Israel peace treaty and the convening of the Madrid peace conference. Still, the passage of time has brought new challenges and new leaders to deal with them. President Clinton clearly recognizes that Prime Minister Netanyahu was elected to pursue a different vision of peace and security than his predecessors and this will require some adjustment in U.S. public diplomacy; it is no less necessary for Prime Minister Netanyahu, who brings to his post an intimate knowledge of American politics and society, to appreciate the broader U.S. strategic interests in the region, the connection between the Arab-Israeli peace process and the security of the Gulf, and the abiding U.S. interest in a meaningful peace process that moves incrementally but progressively toward a negotiated resolution of the Arab-Israeli conflict. In this regard, the conclusion of the Hebron agreement is an important milestone. Building on that achievement, we believe the United States and the Netanyahu government have the opportunity to deepen their cooperation and coordination in the pursuit of regional peace and security.

Economic Partnership. In light of the enormous economic achievements Israel has witnessed in recent years, aided by U.S. economic assistance and the provision of U.S. loan guarantees, the Study Group believes that the United States and Israel are ready to move into a new era in their economic relationship, transforming the donor-recipient connection into a more mature partnership. To assist Israel in the process of achieving full economic independence, important steps should be taken now.

Washington should actively support the Netanyahu government's vision of an Israeli economy driven by the free market, committed to privatization, deregulation, land-tenure reform, and Israel's version of "reinventing government." In addition, the United States should take measures to promote "trade," not "aid," encouraging U.S. investment in Israel and joint U.S.-Israeli initiatives (especially in the defense sector) and taking full advantage of the opportunities afforded by the U.S.-Israel Free Trade Area.

As Prime Minister Netanyahu has stated, a frank and open discussion between Washington and Jerusalem about weaning Israel off U.S. economic assistance is long overdue. This discussion should be driven not just by U.S. budget constraints—which are real and pressing—but by the belief that an end to U.S. economic assistance to Israel will leave

U.S.-Israeli relations on a sounder footing. While the delicacy of the peace process and the burdens of dealing with multiple threats may require a number of years before that goal is reached, our two countries should recognize it as a firm objective, progress toward which would provide a clear measurement of our bilateral relationship. These discussions should commence as soon as possible, with the first steps toward altering the shape and size of U.S. economic assistance to Israel implemented within the next two years.

Charting a path for Israel's "economic independence" (to use Prime Minister Netanyahu's phrase) requires an understanding of the components of the U.S.-Israel aid relationship. The U.S. aid package to Israel includes $1.8 billion in military assistance, much of it used to purchase U.S. arms and matériel, and $1.2 billion in economic assistance (Economic Support Funds or ESF). These allocations have remained unchanged since 1986; as a result of inflation, their value in "constant dollars" has diminished by 30 percent. Of the $1.2 billion in ESF, approximately $1 billion actually goes toward repayment to the United States of loans to Israel for military procurement and construction from the Camp David era. This means that, in reality, 95 percent of the $3 billion total is directly related to security expenditure by Israel. At current funding levels, it will be the year 2010 before $1 billion in economic assistance is *not* directed toward repayment of those military debts. (The military debt, which was transformed from government-to-government debt into a government-to-private sector debt several years ago, will be fully paid off by 2015.) Year by year, however, as that debt is repaid, the proportion of economic support freed up from paying that debt is rising.

In light of this situation, we see several options available for beginning to revamp the aid program now:

- *Transfer ESF not used for debt service into military assistance, where the funds could be targeted to help Israel deal more directly with the unconventional security threats it will face, especially in anti-missile defense.* This could be done within the context of the existing aid package or by setting up a special account which Israel could draw upon as events warrant.

- *Apply those ESF monies to enlarge binational endowments such as the U.S.-Israel Binational Research and Development Fund (BIRD); the Binational Agriculture Research and Development Foundation (BARD); and the Binational Science Fund (BSF) or to expand the focus of the U.S.-Israel Science and Technology Commission.* These examples of joint support for research and development have been shown to be cost-effective forms of foreign assistance; at the same time, they have provided tangible benefit to the American economy— especially in the form of jobs.

- *Re-target those ESF monies to a special "Middle East peace fund" to support multilateral peacemaking efforts, the Middle East Development Bank, and assistance to Israel's peace partners.* This fund could support the efforts of innovative but underfunded programs such as *Builders for Peace*, which encourages private American citizens to invest in the Palestinian areas. Moreover, this fund could be used to leverage other funding that assists private investment in the territories.

- *Deduct those ESF monies directly from overall economic assistance.* This would effectively tie the amount of annual ESF to Israel's debt, so that Israel's annual ESF never exceeds the amount of military debt repayment due each year.

Various members of the Study Group see benefits in each of these options, any of which should be viewed as a first step toward the eventual elimination of the economic assistance program, which we support. Through these initiatives, the United States has the opportunity to advance a U.S.-Israel economic relationship based on shared free-market values and a determination to modernize Israel's economy and support private investment. Such a strategy will promote Israel's economic growth, reduce its economic dependence on the United States, and strengthen our bilateral partnership as we work together to confront our common threats and advance our common interests.

Strategic Cooperation. In the post-Cold War world, the United States and Israel face similar, though not identical, threats from radical regimes, terrorist groups, and the proliferation of weapons of mass destruction and missile delivery systems; a particularly potent new threat is the potential use of WMDs by terrorist groups. Confronting these threats requires enhanced strategic cooperation. Here, we believe it would be more effective for the two parties to build on the existing frameworks of strategic cooperation[1] than to expend political energy on the negotiation of a mutual defense treaty, as proposed by some in Washington and Jerusalem. While such a pact would formalize America's commitment to Israel, thereby enhancing Israeli deterrence, we are more impressed with the drawbacks of this proposal. These include the potential erosion of Israel's ethos of self-reliance, which has always contributed to America's willingness to support it in times of crisis, as well as the difficulty of defining against whom such a treaty would be directed and under what circumstances it would be activated.

Without codifying our relationship in treaty form, there is still much that can be done to enhance our strategic cooperation. Here, the U.S. commitment to maintaining Israel's "qualitative edge" is critical. In the past, that has meant keeping Israel sufficiently strong that it could deter and, if necessary, repulse any conventional threat. In recent years—and especially since Israel suffered from the Scud missile attacks launched by Saddam Hussein during the Gulf War—the definition of "qualitative edge" has been expanded to include nonconventional threats as well. Given the heightened concern about proliferation, with numerous Middle Eastern countries—friends and adversaries alike—investing their limited budgets in WMD programs as a way to compensate for shortfalls in procurement of conventional weaponry, we believe joint counter-proliferation efforts must be given even greater attention.

Specifically, we urge the two governments not only to continue joint research and development of the ARROW anti-ballistic missile program but to expand efforts to develop standardized, interoperable and effective defense systems against tactical ballistic missiles, cruise missiles and aircraft. In addition, we urge Israel's full integration into a

---

[1] These include high-level, institutionalized strategic dialogues such as the Joint Political Military Group and the Joint Strategic Assessment Group, which complement frequent exchanges among cabinet-level officials.

U.S. space-based regional or global system providing instant warning of ballistic missile launching; we commend the recent initiative to provide Israel with greater coverage from our reconnaissance satellites, which is one means to substantially bolster Israeli security without significant new funding. By enhancing Israel's active defense capability, such cooperation contributes to reducing Israeli reliance on prevention and preemption, thus boosting regional stability. Elsewhere, the United States and Israel should enhance their consultations regarding the broader aspects of counter-proliferation, defense planning for contingencies that involve reversals in the peace process that lead to renewed Arab threats to Israeli security; aggressive attempts by Iraq or Iran to intimidate other regional states; and deterioration of the internal security of states whose stability is central to both Israeli and U.S. interests. Finally, the United States and Israel should pursue various forms of "triangular cooperation" with third countries—e.g., Turkey and Jordan—to build upon a congruence of interests in such areas as counter-terrorism and counter-proliferation.

Strategic dialogue between the two countries should clarify a partnership in which each party bears responsibilities to the other. As a general rule, the United States ought to help limit risks to Israel's security by making available appropriate weaponry and technology. Specifically, this entails a commitment to share with Israel, under adequate safeguards, technology whose prohibitive cost prevents Israel from developing it alone. This includes technology designed to respond to surface-to-surface missile threats. On Israel's part, partnership entails a commitment to safeguard this technology and satisfy American sensitivities on the issue of high-tech transfer.

As both the American and the Israeli "home front" have become the targets of spectacular terrorist outrages, sometimes perpetrated by like-minded groups and organizations with similar sinister goals, the fight against terrorism—especially WMD terrorism—deserves special status on the agenda of strategic cooperation. Much more effort must be dedicated to public awareness about—and international cooperation against—such threats as the use of chemical or biological weapons against civilian populations. The recent inauguration of a joint dialogue on counter-terrorism is useful to institutionalize ongoing intelligence exchange and discussion of technical requirements.

Egypt: Restoring the Partnership

For two decades, the U.S.-Egyptian relationship has been a centerpiece of U.S. efforts to bolster peace and security in the Middle East. This reflects Egypt's dominance in Arab political, military, diplomatic and cultural circles. As a result, the seismic shift undertaken by Egypt in the mid-1970s—away from alliance with the Soviets and toward partnership with the United States, away from rejectionism and toward peace with Israel, away from Nasserite socialism and toward a more open economy at home, away from an authoritarian political system and toward the beginning of a more democratic system of government—has had profound ramifications on the international, Middle Eastern and Arab levels.

Those four elements—strategic alliance, commitment to peace, pursuit of economic reforms, and incremental steps toward liberalization and democratization—have been the foundation of the U.S.-Egyptian relationship ever since. Strategically, a shared understanding of the complex challenges facing the region in the post-Cold War world led Cairo to be an early supporter of the U.S.-led alliance to evict Saddam Hussein from Kuwait. On the peace process, Egypt's meticulous implementation of the security components of its peace treaty with Israel has greatly reduced (if not removed) the threat of coalition warfare against Israel and given Israelis the confidence to take risks for peace on other fronts. Along the way, Egypt paid a steep price for its moderation and realism, suffering political isolation, cultural ostracism and lost financial assistance from other Arab donor states. Economically, U.S. assistance partially offset the loss of Arab aid; in the early and mid-1980s, it helped rebuild an infrastructure falling apart under the weight of the twin challenges of overpopulation and underinvestment; more recently, U.S. aid has given Egypt a vital cushion to compensate for difficult reforms that are needed to build a healthier, more dynamic and more entrepreneurial economy. At the core of the U.S. aid effort is the belief that U.S. interests are served by a strong Egypt, able to meet the needs of its people and assert itself on the regional stage.

Over the past few years, public discord and private frustration between Egypt and the United States have increased. At times, these tensions reflect clear policy differences based on the national interests of the two countries; at other times they mirror broader frustration within the two societies. These frustrations—which have affected each of the four core elements of the relationship— have the worrying potential for eroding the foundation of the bilateral relationship. Divergences have emerged over a wide range of Egyptian policies: from Egypt's role in the peace process (both bilateral and multilateral tracks); to the "warmth" (or lack thereof) of Egypt's own relationship with Israel; to relations with terror-supporting states on its borders (especially Libya); to criticism of Israeli-Turkish security ties; to support for Iraqi re-integration into the Arab world; to leadership of the group which opposed the indefinite extension of the Nuclear Nonproliferation Treaty and Cairo's own policies on ballistic missile proliferation. Domestically, the United States is concerned about the set-backs to democratization and human rights as the Egyptian government has moved assertively to contain internal dissent and root out violence on the part of religious extremists. While important areas of U.S.-Egyptian cooperation remain intact, they may reflect only an episodic convergence of interests, not a pattern of partnership.

The Study Group believes that special attention must be devoted to building a true strategic partnership between the United States and Egypt that reflects the realities of the 1990s, not the lingering memories of the 1970s. While the U.S.-Egypt relationship has many of the attributes of a partnership—large-scale military and economic assistance, joint military exercises, frequent high-level political meetings and diplomatic exchanges—the sum does not equal the individual parts. Though the two sides share a common appreciation of the *domestic* threat that terrorism, radicalism and religious militancy can pose to Egyptian stability, we may no longer share a common assessment of *regional* priorities, challenges, threats and opportunities, let alone a common regional agenda.

As a first step toward remedying this, we urge the following:

- *Creation of ongoing, high-level, bilateral consultations on political, strategic, and military matters.* These consultations would provide structure for a relationship that has evolved in an *ad hoc* form despite more than twenty years of contact. In addition, they would provide a forum to vet ideas, share opinions, and air differences without losing sight of the overwhelming mutual interest in advancing the Middle East peace process and maintaining regional security. Over the past three years, the two countries have made impressive progress on promoting private-sector investment and market reforms within the context of a high-level commission of public officials and private sector leaders operating under the chairmanship of President Mubarak and Vice President Gore. That level of partnership needs to be extended to other areas of the bilateral relationship. Indeed, institutionalizing full, frank and candid discussions at all levels of government with our Egyptian partners, complemented by private U.S.-Egyptian dialogues among businessmen, analysts and scholars, is an important way to deepen the U.S.-Egypt relationship and thereby improve U.S.-Egyptian cooperation.

Just as Egyptian support for Desert Shield/Storm was critical in 1990-91, so too is Egyptian acquiescence in—if not active support for—the assertive policy toward Saddam Hussein's regime that the Study Group outlined above. Similarly, in the peace process, Egypt plays a much more constructive role—especially *vis-à-vis* its guardianship role of the Palestinians—when it is consulted and encouraged to contribute its good offices, wherever possible. While Egyptian encouragement of U.S. initiatives may not be essential to their success, Egyptian opposition can often pose difficult obstacles, as evidenced by Egypt's role in Israeli-Palestinian diplomacy in recent months. Recognizing that reality and working it to the advantage of our common interests in regional peace and security should be a top priority.

- *Developing a common agenda and mission for the U.S.-Egyptian security relationship.* The security relationship is important to both parties, as evidenced in the Gulf War. But it is important that the security relationship emerge from a common appreciation of regional threats and challenges. That is why the shape and composition of the $1.3 billion annual U.S. military assistance package should be the product of thorough, ongoing consultations that reflect common approaches to dealing with the dominant threats to regional security. This should include detailed discussions regarding defense planning for contingencies that involve reversals in the peace process so as to protect against the renewed prospects of war; aggressive attempts by Iraq or Iran to intimidate other regional states; and deterioration of the internal security of states whose stability is central to both Egyptian and U.S. interests.

In this context, we strongly urge that Egypt's leaders cease making public statements or taking actions (such as military maneuvers) which characterize Israel as a threat to Egyptian national security. This not only helps poison the atmosphere for Egyptian-Israeli relations and the Arab-Israeli peace process, but it also contributes to deepening concern among officials in both the Executive and Legislative Branches about the direction of Egyptian strategic thinking.

One way to strengthen the U.S.-Egypt security relationship and inject additional content into it is through the establishment of a special U.S.-Egypt working group on counter-terrorism. This is one area in which the two parties' have strong common interests (as evidenced by Egypt's hosting of the Sharm el-Sheikh Summit in March 1996 and U.S.-Egyptian cooperation in combating radical Islamic extremism) that may be useful in attenuating their divergent positions elsewhere (such as their differing approaches to Libya and Sudan).

- *Restructuring the economic relationship to promote a free market and U.S. private investment.* For Cairo and Washington, the objective should be to build an economic relationship as mature and strong as their military relationship that will *inter alia* contribute to economic growth and reduce an important source of societal discontent and potential internal instability. Given the great strides Egypt has taken in structural reform in recent years, coupled with the impending completion of most AID-financed infrastructure projects in the country, now is the time to reshape the $815 million economic assistance package to bolster the process of reform, cut back the huge AID bureaucracy in Cairo, and place the bilateral relationship on a healthier footing.[2] As President Mubarak has publicly recognized, this will entail reductions in U.S. economic assistance—not in pique and not solely in response to U.S. budget considerations, but to derive greater and longer-lasting benefit for Egypt from U.S. aid at lower cost. With this objective in mind, we urge the administration to explore the following options:

  — *Debt Restructuring.* Egypt still owes the U.S. government $5.7 billion in old ESF and PL-480 loans, the debt service of which will be between $350 million and $450 million per year for the next 20 years. The United States could lessen this long-term financial burden by channeling a significant portion of current ESF funds to restructuring this debt to reflect its real market value.

  — *Increased Trade.* The U.S.-Egypt trade balance overwhelmingly favors the United States. This is the result of many factors, including high levels of U.S. assistance, lack of exportable Egyptian goods, and U.S. trade barriers. Building on the promising work of the Gore-Mubarak Commission, Washington and Cairo must together commit themselves to increase bilateral trade and lessen this imbalance. Options to explore include a possible bilateral or regional free

---

[2] As with Israel's assistance package, aid to Egypt has also remained unchanged since 1986; as a result of inflation, its value has diminished by 30 percent in constant dollars.

trade agreement, lowering U.S. trade barriers more rapidly, and additional support for privatization and post-privatization programs, such as capital market development. One innovative idea popular among Egyptian businessmen is to decrease economic assistance via a dollar-for-dollar trade off that matches cuts in aid with increased access to the U.S. market for Egyptian goods, especially textiles, that are currently restricted.

— *Changing the Mix.* This could involve deep cuts in the AID bureaucracy in Cairo with the transfer of some of the "saved money" to Egypt in the form of direct economic assistance, not project assistance. This would lower the overall amount of assistance but give Egypt the power to channel it according to its own wishes, reflecting the growing maturity of the bilateral economic relationship.

The Study Group underscores the importance of shoring up the foundation of the U.S.-Egyptian relationship. Indeed, without Egypt as a full partner, the United States will be handcuffed in its effort to secure its wider interests in regional peace and stability. Many observers, however, view the rift between Washington and Cairo as already so deep and structural that the United States should consider punitive steps, such as cutting U.S. economic or military assistance. Cuts for that reason are wrong and counter-productive; but cuts over time carefully designed to strengthen the long-term prospect for Egyptian political stability and economic prosperity are right and we endorse them.

At the same time, we underscore the need for Egypt to take action to strengthen bilateral relations with the objective of correcting the image of the U.S.-Egyptian relationship as one of only periodic confluence of interests, not strategic partnership. Two areas where Egypt's political weight in the Arab world are crucial to U.S. interests are the maintenance of international sanctions on Iraq and the promotion of Arab normalization with Israel. Egyptian leadership in support of U.S. positions on these issues would go far toward repairing frayed relations; indeed, it is never too late for Egypt to warm its peace with Israel and for President Mubarak to finally end his fifteen-year boycott (except for the special circumstance of Prime Minister Rabin's funeral) and visit Israel. If, however, the gulf between U.S. and Egyptian positions widens, this could bring about the very breach in relations the Study Group fears is possible but hopes to avoid.

Saudi Arabia and the GCC: Deepening Stability and Security

The United States and countries of the Gulf Cooperation Council—especially Saudi Arabia—view the future of their relationship in the second half of the 1990s with a sense of caution and wariness that does not accurately reflect their successful joint efforts to protect Gulf security in the first half of the decade. Iraq's invasion of Kuwait in 1990 had capped more than a decade of profound challenge to the security of the Gulf, that began with the Islamic revolution in Iran and continued with the Soviet invasion of Afghanistan, the Iran-Iraq War, and the "tanker war" in the Gulf. Since 1990, when the United States discarded its "balance of power" approach, led a global coalition against Iraq, and then defined a "containment" strategy to protect Gulf security after evicting Saddam from Kuwait, the Gulf has enjoyed a lengthy period of relative quiet and stability. Though different states view their security situation differently—with southern Gulf states, like Bahrain and the UAE, principally concerned about the creeping threat from Iran and northern Gulf states, like Kuwait, fixated on the threat from Iraq—all recognize that they are more secure today as a result of U.S. steadfastness than they were six years ago.

That reality, however, does not mask the profound unease with key elements of U.S. containment strategy that reverberates throughout the Gulf, with negative implications for the domestic stability of Gulf states. This includes (paradoxically) deepening anxiety over unilateral U.S. actions against Iran and Iraq and over the strength, resilience and staying-power of the U.S. commitment to protect against Iraq and Iran; heightened tensions over the domestic political ramifications of the expanded presence of

U.S. forces on Gulf soil; and rising concern over U.S. burden-sharing initiatives and the high cost of defense against external threats.

While these fears are real, they have emerged against a backdrop of more fundamental political, economic, social and cultural pressures within Arab societies in the Gulf that are the product of the long-term decline in the price of oil, which is the chief (and, in some cases, virtually the only) source of revenue these states enjoy. (In Saudi Arabia and Kuwait, the steady decline in real oil revenues was exacerbated by the huge drain on foreign assets caused by the need to finance the Gulf War.) Today, governments throughout the region are facing growing budget deficits, booming populations, rising unemployment, and a set of socio-economic expectations that will be extremely difficult, if not impossible, to meet.

While each country faces its own unique set of problems—from terrorism in Saudi Arabia, to ethnic and religious strife in Bahrain, to the threat of Iraqi aggression against Kuwait, to the potential for Iranian military confrontation with the UAE—they all share an abiding concern about domestic stability, regional security, how they will manage the competing demands of each, and how they are going to pay for it. Given the closeness of U.S. political, strategic and economic ties with these states, their problems are, in many ways, our problems, too. This was particularly evident in the terrorist bombings against U.S. military installations in Riyadh and Dhahran and the mass anti-government protests that have rocked Bahrain, home to the headquarters of the U.S. Fifth Fleet.

Recalling the core U.S. interests in the Gulf—to prevent any disruption of oil or gas supplies, to promote the stability of those friendly regional states which help provide access to energy resources, and to deter any unfriendly country, ideology or movement from exercising control over the region's energy resources—we urge the following policies to help put these problems on a path toward resolution, thereby strengthening relations with Saudi Arabia and our other GCC partners:

- *The United States should deepen dialogue with Gulf states on the sustainability of the U.S. military presence and on rationalizing Gulf defense expenditures.* The United States should propose detailed discussions on burden-sharing arrangements to determine the practical requirements for sustaining a long-term presence of U.S. forces in Gulf waters and on Gulf soil. The basic elements of an understanding between the United States and GCC countries are clear: as long as Iraq, Iran or any other potential hegemonic power threatens the security of the Gulf and access to the region's energy resources, the United States will stand ready to deter those threats. Current U.S. deterrence strategy relies on three components: inter-Arab security cooperation, bilateral U.S. security relationships with individual Gulf states, and the forward deployment of U.S. forces in the Gulf region. While recognizing the overriding need to maintain a robust deterrent posture, the United States should restrict the location and size of U.S. forces deployed inside the region's historically closed societies. In return, the United States would expect Gulf states to pay for their own defense, to continue to build their own defense capabilities, and to provide facilities required for U.S. forces to fulfill their mission. These steps are essential to sustain U.S. popular support for engagement in the Gulf and to protect against the perception that the United States is more interested in protecting the Gulf than GCC states themselves.

  Here, it is important for the United States to balance its desire to have Gulf countries carry the financial burden of Gulf security against the U.S. interest in the economic well-being of these countries. While Gulf states must bear their full share of expenses, they need to be encouraged to look realistically at their military needs and the importance of absorbing past purchases as they contemplate making new ones. This means the United States should not advise Gulf states to purchase equipment when they cannot afford to do so, but we should work closely with those Gulf states that have adequate resources to improve their own defenses against threats to our common interests.

- *The United States should initiate a high-level dialogue with Saudi Arabia and other Gulf states—individually and collectively—on the need for economic and social reform.* Washington should take the lead in urging its GCC allies to evaluate the demographic, economic and social challenges they face and the need to devise policies that deal with these problems urgently and comprehensively. Our view is that Gulf states only stand a chance of overcoming the long-term domestic challenges to their stability if they pursue a program of structural economic reform, sound financial management, cuts in cradle-to-grave social-welfare spending and subsidy programs, and curbs on corruption that cumulatively cost Gulf economies billions of dollars. If history is any guide, implementing these changes will, at first, exacerbate popular discontent, provoke opposition and perhaps even lead to violence. If Gulf regimes are committed to a process of real economic reform and maintain their commitment in the face of popular opposition, we should extend to them our political and moral support. In this context, we should offer our advice to them that expanding opportunities for popular participation in governance can be a useful way to gain legitimacy for painful economic reform programs; our role as defender of Gulf security—proven in war—gives us special standing to commend economic and social reforms without alienating our partner-states in the process. We should not, however, condition our relationship with them on their progress toward democratic reform and the expansion of human rights. Ever mindful of our commitment to U.S. values, our wider strategic interests dictate that U.S. priorities must be the achievement of stability first, the advancement of democracy second.

- *Injecting realism and balance into America's understanding of Saudi domestic stability.* Because of its status as the dominant player in the global energy market, the leading power in the GCC, and a relative moderate in inter-Arab politics, the United States has a special interest in the security and stability of Saudi Arabia. Confirmed in numerous Presidential statements, this commitment was amply manifested in the dispatch to

Saudi soil of a half-million American troops in 1990-91 and is reaffirmed each day by the deployment of U.S. troops at remote Saudi bases. After the events of the last six years, there should be no doubt about the strength of the U.S. commitment and the resolve to back it up.

What makes this situation so unusual is the imbalance between our commitment to Saudi Arabia's external security and our ignorance about challenges to Saudi domestic security. Indeed among the countries in the world whose security the United States is pledged to defend, U.S. officials probably know the least about events inside Saudi Arabia. In the past, when the Saudi kingdom faced only episodic threats to its internal stability, such as the takeover of the Grand Mosque at Mecca, reconciling this imbalance was neither too difficult nor too troubling. Today, however, circumstances have changed. For the first time in memory, there is genuine concern in U.S. policy circles about the political fate of the Saudi kingdom. That is because three trends appear to have converged at once: uncertainty and perhaps disputes within the ruling family over key issues (e.g., succession, strategic planning, Arab politics); the lack of adequate revenue to maintain a well-lubricated social-welfare system that ensures domestic tranquility; and the emergence of an Islamic opposition that challenges the claim to religious orthodoxy that is the essence of Saudi political legitimacy. While we do not believe that the Saudis face an imminent threat to their security, the fact that oppositionists—be they Sunni or Shi'i—have succeeded in two terrorist attacks against U.S. installations in or near Saudi urban centers is deeply troubling; the additional fact that Saudi authorities have been reluctant to extend their full cooperation to U.S. agencies investigating these crimes is even more so. It was this sense of concern that recently prompted the Central Intelligence Agency to establish a special task force dedicated to following Saudi domestic developments.

While Washington should not sound an exaggerated alarm about Saudi instability that might itself constitute a self-fulfilling prophecy, it should not be sanguine about Saudi domestic security and the Saudis' ability to grapple with multiple security challenges simultaneously. The

United States needs to learn more about events and trends within Saudi society and to seek out new avenues, beyond the traditional channels of diplomatic contact, to deepen its knowledge base. This is essential if we are to offer informed advice to our Saudi allies and to safeguard our stake in Saudi stability.

In addition, the United States should impress upon the Saudis the necessity of their full cooperation in two key areas: policy toward Iraq and counter-terrorism. Any lessening of Saudi resolve in support of U.S. regional security efforts or the lack of full and unconditional cooperation in the prevention and investigation of terrorist attacks against U.S. citizens, assets and interests would be sure to erode support for the U.S. commitment to Saudi security. In particular, nothing will damage popular support for this commitment more than a decision by the Saudis to withhold information about past or future terrorist attacks or an attempt to skew that information to serve other political interests.

Turkey: Underscoring Core Interests and Values

In its diplomacy toward Turkey, the United States faces a difficult and complex challenge: an unfriendly leader at the helm of the government of an allied regime. The good news for Washington is that Prime Minister Necmettin Erbakan's power in foreign affairs and security issues is constrained by the ongoing influence of Turkey's pro-Western forces; moreover, the coalition government he heads holds only a narrow parliamentary majority that could evaporate on short notice. The bad news is that—whatever government may be in power in Ankara—the U.S.-Turkish alliance that developed during the Cold War today suffers from post-Cold War differences over regional policy and human rights concerns that have soured ties and threatened the traditionally close bilateral defense relationship.

As head of the Islamist Refah Party, which favors a gradual rollback of Turkey's seventy-year experiment in secularism, Erbakan in opposition had a history of vituperatively anti-American and anti-Western pronouncements, including opposition to Turkey's defense relationship with the United States and NATO. As prime minister, however, Erbakan is not totally a free agent. President Suleyman Demirel, a staunch secularist, retains considerable authority. Erbakan himself leads a narrow-majority coalition in partnership with Tansu Çiller, who heads a right-of-center, pro-Western party and serves as deputy prime minister and foreign minister. His foreign policy flexibility also is circumscribed by the traditionally powerful National Security Council. This ten-member body consists of the top five civilian officials and the top five military officers; of that group, all but Erbakan are staunchly pro-Western and pro-secular.

Aware that he must move gradually and avoid crossing any of the military's "red lines"—Erbakan-led parties twice were banned following military interventions into government—Erbakan has described the United States as a "friend and ally." He has not assaulted the basic tenets of Turkey's defense relationship with the West, but he has consistently rankled Washington with his actions and words, such as his natural gas-pipeline deal with Iran (signed within days of the passage of the Iran-Libya Sanctions Act), his stated interest in "defense industrial cooperation" with Iran, his visit to Libya (during which he implicitly accused the United States of "terrorism") and his accusation that the United States initially intended to use Operation Provide Comfort to establish an independent Kurdish state in southeastern Turkey.

In light of the deep divisions which characterize Turkish politics and the importance Washington attaches to Turkey's role as a Muslim democracy and Western ally at the meeting point of Europe, Central Asia and the Middle East, dealing with an Erbakan-led Turkey is a particularly sensitive task. We believe it can be best pursued through a *dual-track policy* toward Turkey, subtly executed, that reflects abiding U.S. interests in a stable, democratic, free-market, secular-oriented Turkey and that implicitly distinguishes between friend and foe. This policy should be guided by the following principles:

- *The United States should focus its diplomacy toward Turkey on the key issues in the bilateral relationship and avoid playing Turkish domestic politics.* We should judge and react to Erbakan and his government mainly according to what they do that affects our fundamental interests. As long as Turkey continues to fulfill its NATO and bilateral defense obligations, we need not get too agitated about, much less assume an overtly hostile posture toward, this government. Of course, when its words or actions are offensive or contrary to U.S. interests, we should respond accordingly; indeed, the United States should hold the Erbakan government to the standards expected of a Western ally, in both word and deed. This applies to the numerous areas where Turkish policy touches on key U.S. interests in the Middle East—from Turkish overtures to Iran and Libya, to Turkey's role in containing Saddam and maintaining security in northern Iraq, to Turkey's attitude toward Israel and the peace process.

- *At the same time, the United States should not shrink from advocating its traditional support for Western values as a key component of the U.S.-Turkish relationship.* It is clear that the most serious threat that an Islamist-led Turkey poses to long-term U.S.-Turkish relations—the potential for a fundamental shift of the Turkish state away from a secular, pro-Western orientation—can only be dealt with effectively by Turks. At the same time, however, we must recognize that our actions toward Erbakan and the Turkish government will have domestic ramifications inside Turkey. Therefore, it is important to maintain traditional U.S. support for the forces of secularism, democracy, and a pro-Western orientation in the only democracy in the Muslim Middle East.

- *Recognizing the central role that the Turkish military plays as guardian of the country's pro-Western orientation, we believe that maintaining a strong U.S.-Turkish security relationship is critical. This will require Executive Branch leadership in convincing Congress about the overriding importance of security ties in the overall U.S.-Turkish relationship.* This includes affirming Turkey's access to the U.S. arms market, which is particularly crucial for retaining bilateral defense relations in an era when foreign aid has dwindled to historically low levels. The recent record highlights the urgency of the problem. In 1996, Congress approved a meager $25 million in ESF funds for Turkey and conditioned that amount on Turkey's lifting of its alleged blockade on Armenia and its recognition of the Armenian genocide; Ankara rejected the terms and turned down the aid. On military supply matters, the United States held up Turkey's purchase of ten Cobra attack helicopters for so long that the exasperated Turks withdrew the order; in addition, a congressional "hold" on the release of three frigates that President Clinton publicly promised to President Demirel has prevented Turkey from taking delivery of items that it has already leased and paid for. This trend is deeply destructive to the long-term health of the U.S.-Turkish relationship; given the domestic politics involved, resolving this problem may require Presidential intervention.

Beyond a supply relationship, bilateral defense cooperation should also include U.S. initiatives to deepen dialogue on counter-proliferation and counter-terrorism, reflecting Turkey's growing concern about these issues based on its location along the border of three known "proliferators" and terror-supporting states: Iraq, Iran and Syria.

Human rights—which tend to dominate congressional interest in Turkey—must be an important element of our bilateral dialogue and the Turkish establishment needs fully to understand Western concerns and the stakes for Turkey's ties with the West. For maximum effect, however, this dialogue should be conducted in a low-visibility manner, designed to achieve results more than headlines. Moreover, concern about human rights should not be allowed to overwhelm bilateral relations.

• *Precisely because of the challenge posed by an Islamist-led Turkey, the U.S. interest in anchoring the Turkish state more firmly to the West has assumed added importance. As a result, the United States should actively support closer ties between Turkey and Western Europe.* U.S. support for Turkish entry into a customs union with the European Union in 1995 established the precedent of U.S. diplomatic involvement in EU-Turkish relations. Now, we should emphasize to the EU the importance of implementing all its commitments made to Turkey when it entered the customs union, especially the payment of more than $350 million in structural adjustment and other transition funds that have been held up reportedly due to Greek opposition and the European Parliament's concern over human rights. These EU policies serve the domestic political interests of Mr. Erbakan, who opposed customs union while in the opposition and could use the EU's withholding of funds as an excuse to withdraw Turkey from the agreement. Washington should press Athens and other EU capitals to lift the hold on these funds.

More generally, the United States should urge EU capitals to keep the door open to eventual EU membership for Turkey, which was a faithful NATO ally throughout the Cold War. Turks are already deeply suspicious that they are being excluded from the EU on the basis of religion; shutting the door on EU membership would confirm it. "Keeping the door open" does not mean that Turkey should be admitted to full EU membership before it meets all the relevant criteria; for now, it clearly falls short in both political and economic qualifications. We should, however, urge our EU partners to treat Turkey equally with countries now on the "first tier" waiting list, which includes virtually every non-EU, Christian European state. Current EU policy, in effect, defines Europe in a way that excludes Turkey. That can only serve the anti-Western ends of Turkey's Islamist movement, which feeds on the anger and frustration bred by Western rejection.[3]

- *In Middle East affairs, the United States should make clear its support for Turkish-Israeli defense and economic cooperation, as embodied in five agreements signed in 1996.* This cooperation

---

[3] In December 1996, Erbakan refused an invitation to join EU leaders for dinner during the EU summit in Dublin, complaining that he would only attend if Turkey were invited to all the summit events (as other EU "waiting list" states were). Some Turks saw his excuse as a ruse behind which to pursue his anti-Western agenda and criticized his non-attendance. But many others, including many secularists, were heartened by his assertion of national pride and resistance to "European anti-Turkish discrimination."

between two U.S. allies—and the region's two democracies—is a "wedge issue" inside Turkey, separating much of the Turkish secular establishment from the Islamists. Its success would hearten and embolden the country's pro-Western military, which so far has withstood efforts by Erbakan to slow or even freeze cooperation with Israel.

Turkey's battle against terrorism perpetrated by the Kurdish Workers Party (PKK) deserves Washington's political support as well as intelligence and counter-terrorism cooperation. Given Syria's patronage of the PKK, an important signal of U.S. support to Turkey would be a clarification of U.S. policy toward Syria's potential removal from the list of terror-supporting states. *We urge the administration to confirm publicly that a cessation of all forms of support to the PKK and other anti-Turkish terrorist groups is a necessary prerequisite for Syria's removal from the "terrorism list"—regardless of Syrian actions on the Arab-Israeli peace process.*

- *On Iraq, Turkey's role is vital.* In 1990, the decision by then-President Turgut Ozal to support the Gulf War alliance unreservedly was a critical element in the coalition's success; today, Turkish cooperation in implementing UN sanctions on Iraq and in working for stability in northern Iraq is similarly crucial. This year, Washington supported UNSC 986—the "oil-for-food" deal with Iraq—not only to help the Iraqi people but also to address long-standing Turkish complaints that its economy had suffered tremendously due to the embargo on Iraq. In addition, the United States has been quite sympathetic to Turkish efforts to fight terrorism emanating from northern Iraq, including giving tacit approval to Turkish military incursions into the area. In response, the United States has a right to expect Ankara's complete adherence to UN resolutions, coordination in enforcing UN sanctions, and cooperation in responding forcefully to Iraqi provocations and violations of the sanctions regime.

- *Outside the region, the United States should recognize the gravity of the worsening situation between Greece and Turkey, with bilateral tensions at their highest point in years.* Against a backdrop of deep hostility and suspicion, there are three immediate points of friction: efforts by Greece to sour EU-Turkish relations and hold up payment of EU structural adjustment funds to Turkey; territorial disputes over several small Aegean islands, which nearly resulted in hostilities last year; and brewing confrontation over the planned purchase of Russian ground-to-air missiles by Greek ally Cyprus, which threatens Turkey's long-standing military dominance on the island and has recently provoked stern Turkish warnings. Beyond the obvious interest Washington has in defusing conflict between two NATO allies, the United States should make a special effort to prevent an escalation of Turkish-Greek tensions lest they permit Erbakan to bolster his populist credentials by making common cause with the Turkish military on an issue of wide nationalist appeal. *The United States should therefore view a diplomatic effort to ease Greek-Turkish tensions as an important priority, pursuing a balanced, even-handed approach which encourages Ankara and Athens to resolve their differences by peaceful means.*

- *In this regard, it is important for the United States, in so far as possible, to adopt an approach that refrains from statements or actions that will redound to the political benefit of Turkey's Islamist movement.* Our goal should be to avoid steps that will assist Erbakan and his colleagues in proving to the Turkish public the viability of their "independent" foreign policy or their brand of populist economics. We should similarly avoid steps that indicate U.S. approval of these policies or U.S. acquiescence in anti-secularist tendencies. Barring a *volte face* in his traditional hostility to the West, the administration should also avoid providing Erbakan with the symbolic victory he would enjoy from visiting Washington.* Throughout, however, it is important that U.S. officials maintain business-like

---

* Dissenting Note: *While supporting the thrust of this policy vis-à-vis Turkey, one Study Group member believes the United States should never attempt to deny the prime minister of a friendly or allied state access to Washington and other forms of relations because the United States opposes his/her ideology. In this instance, denying Erbakan access to Washington is just as likely to strengthen Islamic radicals as to weaken them (Cordesman).*

relations with all arms of the Turkish government, including those ministries headed by Refah partisans.

Differentiating between U.S. support for the Turkish state and our distaste for particular actions and statements of its prime minister and governing party will require a sensitive and difficult balancing act. If carefully implemented, this "dual-track" approach will permit the United States to demonstrate its strategic preferences, while avoiding open declarations of support for any particular party (which would be counter-productive) and eschewing open hostility toward a government that, at least for now, is restraining its own hostility toward Washington. Such an approach to Turkey is likely to remain appropriate as long as Turkey's divided government—half Islamist, half secular— remains in power. Whoever its prime minister may be, however, Turkey's geostrategic importance will remain intact. If, over time, Islamists emerge as clear winners of their tug-of-war with the secularists for control of foreign policy, then the United States will no doubt have to modify its approach. Until then, pursuing this policy is the best means the United States has at its disposal for preventing that from happening.

Members of the
Presidential Study Group

Kenneth Adelman, a nationally syndicated columnist, served as director of the Institute of Contemporary Studies and as director of the Arms Control and Disarmament Agency during the Reagan administration.

Alfred L. Atherton is chairman of Search for Common Ground's Initiative for Peace and Cooperation in the Middle East. He previously served as assistant secretary of state for Near East and South Asian affairs, ambassador-at-large for Middle East negotiations and ambassador to Egypt.

Howard Berman (D-CA) serves on the House International Relations Committee and is ranking member of its Subcommittee on International Operations.

Graeme Bannerman is founder and president of the international consulting firm Bannerman and Associates, Inc. Previously, he served as the staff director for the Senate Foreign Relations Committee.

Deborah Bodlander is a professional staff member for the House International Relations Committee, specializing in the Middle East.

John Bolton is vice president of the American Enterprise Institute. He previously served as assistant secretary of state for international organization affairs in the Bush administration and president of the National Policy Forum.

Anthony Cordesman is co-director of Middle East Studies at the Center for Strategic and International Studies. He has served as assistant for national security to Senator John McCain and in senior positions in the Office of the Secretary of Defense, the State Department, the Department of Energy, and the Defense Advanced Research Projects Agency.

Paula J. Dobriansky is senior international affairs and trade advisor at the law firm of Hunton and Williams. She served as associate director for policy and programs at the U.S. Information Agency, as deputy assistant secretary of state for human rights and humanitarian affairs, and as director of European and Soviet affairs at the National Security Council. She was also a foreign policy advisor for the Dole for President campaign.

Michael Eisenstadt is the military affairs fellow at The Washington Institute and the author, most recently, of *Iranian Military Power: Capabilities and Intentions* (The Washington Institute, 1996). He previously worked as an analyst in the U.S. Army and served as a member of the U.S. Air Force's Gulf War Air Power Survey.

Douglas Feith is a founding member of the law firm Feith and Zell, P.C. During the Reagan administration, he served as deputy assistant secretary of defense for negotiations policy and on the National Security Council staff.

Benjamin Gilman (R-NY) is the chairman of the House International Relations Committee.

Richard Haass, director of foreign policy studies at the Brookings Institution, served from 1989 to 1993 as special assistant to President Bush and senior director for Near East and South Asian affairs at the National Security Council.

Alexander Haig, Jr., chairman of Worldwide Associates, has served as secretary of state, White House chief of staff and NATO supreme commander.

Bruce Jentleson is director of the University of California at Davis Washington Center and former deputy director of the State Department Policy Planning Staff in the Clinton administration.

Max M. Kampelman is chairman of the American Academy of Diplomacy and the Georgetown University Institute for the Study of Diplomacy. Previously, he was counselor of the

Department of State and head of the U.S. delegation to the negotiations on nuclear and space arms in Geneva.

Geoffrey Kemp is director of regional strategic programs at the Nixon Center for Peace and Freedom. He served as special assistant to President Reagan and senior director for Near East and South Asian affairs at the National Security Council.

Zalmay Khalilzad, former deputy assistant secretary of defense in the Bush administration, is the program director for strategy, doctrine, and force structure for the RAND Corporation's Project Air Force and director of RAND's Greater Middle East Studies Center.

Jeane Kirkpatrick, senior fellow at the American Enterprise Institute, served as the permanent U.S. representative to the United Nations during the Reagan administration.

Mel Levine, a partner in the law office of Gibson, Dunn & Crutcher, LLP, served from 1983-93 as a Democratic congressman from California.

Samuel W. Lewis, counselor to The Washington Institute, served as director of the Department of State's Policy Planning Staff in the Clinton administration and as ambassador to Israel under Presidents Carter and Reagan. From 1987 to 1993, he was president of the United States Institute of Peace.

Joseph Lieberman (D-CT) is a member of the Senate Armed Services Committee and chairman of the Democratic Leadership Council.

Alan Makovsky is a senior fellow at The Washington Institute specializing in the Middle East peace process and Turkey. In eleven years at the State Department, he served as division chief for Southern Europe, Bureau of Intelligence and Research; political advisor to Operation Provide Comfort; and special advisor to Special Middle East Coordinator Dennis Ross.

Michael Mandelbaum is the Christian A. Herter Professor of American Foreign Policy at the Johns Hopkins University's Nitze School of Advanced International Studies and director of the Project on East-West Relations at the Council on Foreign Relations.

Will Marshall is president and founder of the Progressive Policy Institute. He was previously policy director of the Democratic Leadership Council.

Robert C. McFarlane, chairman and CEO of McFarlane and Associates, Inc., served as National Security Advisor during the Reagan administration.

Daniel Pipes is editor of the *Middle East Quarterly* and adjunct scholar of The Washington Institute. Among his many published works is *Syria Beyond the Peace Process* (The Washington Institute, 1996.)

Kenneth Pollack, a research fellow at The Washington Institute, served previously as an aide in the Directorate for Near East and South Asian affairs of the National Security Council and as a Persian Gulf military analyst at the Central Intelligence Agency.

Alan Platt, partner at the law firm Gibson, Dunn & Crutcher, served as the Mideast director of the Arms Control and Disarmament Agency.

James Roche is corporate vice president and general manager of the Electronic Sensors and Systems Division of the Northrop Grumman Corporation. In government, he served as Democratic staff director of the Senate Armed Services Committee and as the principal deputy director of the Department of State's Policy Planning Staff.

Peter Rodman, director of national security programs at the Nixon Center for Peace and Freedom, has served in senior national security positions in numerous Republican administrations, including service as the deputy national security advisor during the Reagan administration.

Robert Satloff is executive director of The Washington Institute for Near East Policy. In 1992-93, he served on President-elect Clinton's National Security Transition Team, focusing on the Arab-Israeli peace process.

Harvey Sicherman is president and director of the Foreign Policy Research Institute and adjunct scholar of The Washington Institute. He was a member of the Department of State's Policy Planning Staff during the Reagan and Bush administrations.

Stephen Solarz, visiting professor of international relations at George Washington University, served from 1975-92 as a Democratic congressman from New York.

Steven Spiegel is a professor of political science at the University of California at Los Angeles.

Roscoe Suddarth is president of the Middle East Institute. He previously served as ambassador to Jordan and as deputy assistant secretary of state in the Bureau of Near East Affairs.

Paul Wolfowitz, dean of the Johns Hopkins University's Nitze School of Advanced International Studies, served as undersecretary of defense for policy in the Bush administration and as ambassador to Indonesia.

R. James Woolsey, senior partner at the law firm Shea & Gardner, served as director of central intelligence during the Clinton administration.

Robert Zoellick, executive vice president and general counsel of Fannie Mae, served as counselor of the Department of State and undersecretary of state for economic affairs during the Bush administration.

Mortimer Zuckerman is publisher of *U.S. News and World Report.*

Appendix

The following Study Group members participated in the "strategic dialogues" in Hurghada and Caesaria in July 1996.

Graeme Bannerman
John Bolton
Anthony Cordesman
Douglas Feith
Geoffrey Kemp
Samuel Lewis
Daniel Pipes
Peter Rodman
Robert Satloff
Steven Spiegel
Roscoe Suddarth

Daniel Kurtzer, principal deputy assistant secretary of state for intelligence and research, participated in this trip as an "observer."

Following are the Egyptian participants at the Hurghada retreat:

Nabil Abdel Ghaffar, information department in the Ministry of Foreign Affairs

Tarek Adel, Foreign Minister's cabinet

Mahmoud Abaza, senior official of the Wafd Party

Salah Bassiouny, former ambassador to the Soviet Union and former director of the Diplomatic Institute

Ahmad Gamal Eldin, North American department in the Ministry of Foreign Affairs

Mustafa Elwi, professor, faculty of economics and political science, Cairo University

Nabil Fahmy, minister plenipotentiary and political advisor to the Foreign Minister

Ahmad Fakhr (Maj.-Gen., retired), director of the National Center for Middle East Studies

Muhammad Shafik Gabr, chief executive officer of Artoc Group and president of the American Chamber of Commerce in Egypt

Osama el-Ghazali Harb, chief editor of *International Politics Magazine*

Amr el-Hinawi, protocol department, Ministry of Foreign Affairs

Amr Ramadan, Foreign Minister's cabinet

Abdel Moneim Said Aly, director, al-Ahram Center for Political and Strategic Studies

Muhammad el-Sayed Said, al-Ahram Center for Political and Strategic Studies

Mohammad Sid Ahmad, columnist, *al-Ahram*

Salama Ahmad Salama, columnist, *al-Ahram*

Hamdi Saleh, director, Research Centers Affairs, Foreign Ministry

Sallama Shaker, deputy assistant to the Foreign Minister for American affairs

Following are the Israeli participants in the Caesaria retreat:

Moshe Arens, former defense minister, foreign minister, and ambassador to the United States

Eliahu Ben Elissar, Likud MK, ambassador-designate to the United States and former ambassador to Egypt

Oded Eran, deputy director-general for economics, Ministry of Foreign Affairs

Moshe Fox, head of the North American division, Ministry of Foreign Affairs

Hirsh Goodman, editor-in-chief of the *Jerusalem Report*

Yossi Hadas, former director-general, Ministry of Foreign Affairs

Yisrael Harel, member of the Yesha council, editor of *Nequda* and spokesman for Jewish settlers in the West Bank and Gaza Strip

Ariel Levite, deputy director and head of arms control in the Directorate of Foreign Affairs at the Ministry of Defense

David Makovsky, diplomatic correspondent, *The Jerusalem Post*; special correspondent, *U.S. News and World Report*

Sallai Meridor, head of the Settlements Division, World Zionist Organization

Ori Orr, Labor MK and former head of the Knesset Foreign Affairs and Defense Committee

Ze'ev Schiff, defense editor of *Ha'aretz*

Shabtai Shavit, former head of Israel's external security service, Mossad

Zalman Shoval, former Likud MK and former ambassador to the United States

Ephraim Sneh, Labor MK and former minister of health

Gerald Steinberg, senior research fellow at the Begin-Sadat Center for Strategic Studies at Bar-Ilan University

Asher Susser, former director of the Moshe Dayan Center for Middle Eastern and African Studies, Tel Aviv University

Ehud Ya'ari, chief Middle East correspondent, Israel Television